Maurice Burton's
World of Nature

Published in 1971 by Purnell
© 1971 by B.P.C. Publishing Limited, London W.1.
Printed in Italy
SBN 361 01768 5

Maurice Burton's World of Nature

PURNELL

London

Acknowledgements

The publishers are grateful to the following for permission to use their photographs: Australian News and Information Bureau: pages 19, 28, 29, 73, 74; Barnaby's Picture Library: pages 27, 34, 42, 47, 59, 70, 79, 80, 81, 85; Bruce Coleman Limited: pages 14, 15, 21, 36, 37, 45, 52, 56, 57, 61, 64, 65, 77, 91; "The Lions of Longleat": page 49; National Council of Tourism in Lebanon: page 60; The Natural History Photographic Agency: pages 25, 35, 41, 69, 76, 84, 86; World Wildlife Fund: page 58.

Contents

Introduction

IN THIS Annual we take stock of what has been happening in the natural world, at home and abroad, in recent times. Not long ago we had the first Conservation Year. It is only natural therefore that much of what we have to say will deal with conservation. This alone would not be enough, however. We must look at some of the more recent discoveries, and for full measure we might also take a look at some of the more unusual and curious things which perplex people's minds from time to time.

"Conservation" is from the word "conserve" which means to keep something safe from destruction. It means almost the same thing as to preserve something or to protect something, but there is a slight difference. There was a time not so very long ago when conservation, protection and preservation of our wild life were given much the same meaning. Today we speak of conservation as "wise management of natural resources". These resources may be animal, vegetable or mineral; they may be a beauty spot, or the backyard through which the Town Hall wants to drive a new road. The emphasis must be on the word "wise". To be wise we must acquire knowledge, and much of the damage done in times past—damage we are seeking to repair today—has been a result of ignorance rather than actual brutality.

The word "preservation" should be used when we are talking about an animal or plant that is threatened with extinction. We shall give a few examples of these later on. When we use the word "protection" we are speaking more of species of animals or plants that are threatened, but not necessarily in the immediate future; they could be in need of protection in perhaps ten or twenty years time.

Twenty or thirty years ago, another word, "environment", was seldom used except by scientists. Today it is on everybody's lips. It means the surroundings in which we live.

Again and again we hear it said that one of the main differences between the human race and all other living species is that man can control his environment, while other species cannot. If this is true then the human race as a whole has failed, for we are fast wrecking not only our own environment but that of all living species, as we shall presently see.

Another word which has become almost as commonplace in this century, and especially during the last fifty years, is "ecology". This deals with where animals and plants live, and how they cope with both the physical and chemical factors in their environment and with the other animals and plants in it. Together, these form what is usually called the balance of nature.

Red Letter Years

IN SOME years there have been remarkable discoveries that have hit the headlines. One of these was 1939, when the coelacanth was discovered off the coast of South Africa. This was a fish thought to have been extinct for seventy million years, until it suddenly turned up in a trawl with a catch of ordinary fish. In fact, it was caught on December 22, just before Christmas Day in 1938, but the news of this discovery did not reach the world until January 1939. The coelacanth (pronounced sealacanth) was important because it was what is called a living fossil, a species that has survived into modern times when all its relatives have died out long ago. Even more important, it belonged to a family of fishes that may have been the first to crawl out on to dry land, to give rise to the first salamanders, and through them to the reptiles, birds and mammals. So the first coelacanths could have been man's first ancestors on land. Anyway, photographs of this five-foot-long fish appeared in all the papers. There were articles written on it, radio broadcasts about it, and a book was written about it.

The Second World War broke out in September 1939, so we are apt to forget that 1939 was the year of the coelacanth. The fish was overshadowed by man's own attempt to wipe out much of his own species. This reminds us of another important year in the calendar of animals, 1914. In that year, the first animal species of which we have the exact time of its end became extinct. It was the passenger pigeon of North America. This pigeon was so numerous at one time that it blackened the sky in its millions. It was killed for food in such large numbers that by the early years of this century it had been wiped out in the wild. The last passenger

The coelacanth was possibly man's first ancestor on land

pigeon died in the Cincinatti Zoo, in the United States, at 5 p.m. on September 1, 1914, almost as the first shots were being fired in the First World War, another occasion when man did his best to wipe out his own species. So the passing of the passenger pigeon attracted little attention.

Fortunately, not all red-letter years for animals have to do with a species being wiped out. Some mark the discovery of new species which are found alive after being thought dead, like the coelacanth. On November 20, 1948, a flightless bird, a rail about the size of a farmyard hen, was re-discovered living in a mountain valley in South Island, New Zealand. This was the takahe, which had been believed extinct for fifty years. In 1961, the noisy scrub-bird was re-discovered in Western Australia. It was first discovered in 1842 by John Gilbert but was later thought to have been wiped out, and in 1949 a memorial commemorating both Gilbert and the noisy scrub-bird he had discovered was erected near the spot where, as everyone thought, the bird *used* to live. Then, in 1961, a single bird was seen and in 1963 a nest was found. The noisy scrub-bird is now fully protected by law, and so is the takahe.

Sometimes a year is marked by a totally different kind of discovery. In 1955 a young dolphin was noticed near the shore at Opononi, on North Island, New Zealand. By 1956, Opo, as the dolphin came to be called, had made friends with bathers and would follow boats around, give children rides on its back and play with beach balls and beer bottles people gave it, balancing these

on its snout as it swam with them. Long accounts of Opo's antics appeared in the newspapers; it was photographed and filmed, and people flocked to the seaside town of Opononi to see it. One day, Opo was found dead. It had become wedged among rocks and, being unable to rise to the surface to breathe, it had drowned. As the tide went out its body was discovered, and as it was carried ashore people wept, they thought so much of this playful dolphin.

Now comes a quite remarkable turn to the story. Two thousand years ago Pliny, the Roman naturalist, wrote down the story of a dolphin that made friends with people at the seaside town of Hippo (now called Bizerta) not far from Tunis, on the North African coast. It was almost exactly like the story of Opo, including the way people flocked to Hippo to see the dolphin. The ending was different, however. The town rulers of Hippo were so annoyed at the way people crowded into their streets and on to their beaches to see the dolphin that they gave orders for it to be killed.

Poor Pliny! Ever since he wrote about the Hippo dolphin people have accused him of having told a tall story. Yet he was proved right, two thousand years later, by a friendly dolphin on the other side of the world.

The year 1970 actually did end with a tall story, one that stands no chance of being believed two thousand years hence. It came from Ramsgate, in south-east England, and it told how a dog and a cat had been close companions, and how the dog had had a litter of babies that were half-puppy, half-kitten. Photographs appeared in some

newspapers, and the question was raised whether it was possible for a cat and a dog to mate and produce a family.

Of course, the whole story was pure nonsense and a few days later a photograph was printed of a man laughing his head off. He had confessed that it was all a practical joke. This photograph and one showing the baby animals—which were quite ordinary puppies—were shown on BBC's children's programme *Blue Peter*, when it was said that zoologists all around the country "had been baffled". This remark was far short of the truth.

In fact, the story of the Ramsgate puppies is an old story in a new form. Usually the story is told of a cat and a rabbit that were close friends. Then the cat had a litter of babies that were half-cat, half-rabbit. If ever you hear this story you can be sure that a cat with the usual long tail has had a litter of kittens with stumpy tails, like a rabbit's scut. They are Manx kittens. Every now and

then this kind of thing happens with cat families, more often in some parts of the world than others. When, many years ago, it happened in the Isle of Man a race of cats, the Manx cats, came into being.

When two animals of different species mate and have a family it is known as cross-breeding. The babies are called hybrids. The mule is a hybrid of a horse and a donkey. But a horse and a donkey are closely related, which is why they can cross-breed. A lion and a tiger, two more closely related species, have been known to cross-breed in a zoo. The babies are known as tigons. Species of ducks will cross-breed. They also are close relatives, almost first cousins.

Had a cat and a dog really cross-bred, at Ramsgate, 1970 would have been more than a red-letter year, we should have had the discovery of the century. Indeed, it would have been a miracle.

Although it is difficult to name any really outstanding recent discovery in the wild-life field, there has been a turning point in one respect. It seems as if we have become truly aware for the first time of what we—mankind as a whole—are doing to our environment.

About ten years ago Rachel Carson's book *Silent Spring* created a stir. It was all about how, with chemicals for pesticides, we were poisoning the countryside, and that if this went on we should kill off all the birds. Instead of the chorus of bird-song we enjoy in spring the countryside would be silent.

Many things have happened since then to shock us. We have had alarming stories about radio-active fall-out. There has been the Torrey Canyon disaster, when an oil-ship was wrecked on the south-west coast of England and tons of oil were spilled on to the sea's surface. Much of this oil came ashore and polluted the beaches, killing sea-birds and generally wiping out marine life. In addition to outstanding events of this kind we are constantly reminded, by our newspapers and broadcast programmes, that we are littering our surroundings and polluting the air we breathe, the soil our food is grown in, our rivers and the oceans. We are destroying our beauty spots as well, and ravaging our wildlife. Much of this is happening unseen by us, but recently there came the realization—as never before and by more people than ever before—that what we are all doing now is going to mean that in twenty or thirty years time, if we do not change our habits, the world is going to be spoilt beyond redemption.

Then there came a new alarm. It had

Sewage pollution in Kenya is becoming a serious threat to the lives of the flamingoes

JANE BURTON

nothing to do with fall-out, or organo-chlorides, oil-pollution or any of the other horrors that had been conjured up. It was simply a realization of the dangers that lie in allowing sewage to flow unchecked into the sea, so polluting the ocean far worse than by any other means. For there is no doubt of the effect of sewage. The River Thames once had fine salmon, but as sewage pollution grew the salmon disappeared.

You might think that a country like Kenya would so far have been spared this kind of pollution, for we are apt to think of Kenya as a kind of wildlife paradise (as indeed it is in many ways). Yet we learn that even Kenya has its sewage menace. On Lake Nakuru, for instance, live millions of flamingoes.

The sight of these birds, especially when large flocks take to the air all together, is one of the wonders of the world. But we are told that sewage flowing into this lake may in time kill off all these beautiful birds.

Here, then, is perhaps one of the greatest dangers to our environment; one which must inevitably grow worse, and one about which little has so far been done. Sewage pollution may well make the holiday resorts of the Mediterranean unusable in the future, quite apart from other evils it may cause. And this is a form of pollution that has stolen up on us and taken us unawares, while our eyes have been fixed on pesticides. Sewage pollution has reached even the South Pacific islands, where coral lagoons are becoming fouled. This may have something to do with the crown-of-thorns plague we discuss on another page.

JANE BURTON

Mice, such as these, are among the most obvious invaders of large houses

Squatters in House and Garden

A SHORT while ago a group of girls were set the task of listing the animals they could find living in their houses. The list was a surprisingly long one. The most obvious invader of large houses is the mouse. Indeed, it is called the house mouse to distinguish it from the many other mice living out of doors. Rats also sometimes come into houses. Having dealt with these obvious invaders we can then start up in the roof space, as the girls did, and work downwards into the basements and cellars. The swift and the starling both have the habit of nesting in roof spaces and with them are the various bats. There are also spiders, of which three species in Britain are called house spiders because they are found mainly indoors, although in winter some of the outdoor spiders move in to shelter from the cold weather. Then there are various flies, including the house fly. There is the tiny insect known as the silverfish which we find in the kitchen (especially where bread or flour are stored) or in old books, where they feed on the paste of the bindings. So the list can be extended, of the animals that have taken to living with man. We speak of them as commensals.

From one part of the world to another the story is the same, although the species of animals may differ. In all cases these animals originally lived or sheltered in caves or hollow trees and to them a house is merely a more convenient cave or hollow. To many it also has the advantage that they can find their food there.

The most spectacular of these commensals are the house mouse, the common or brown rat and the ship or black rat. All three are believed to have come originally from central Asia, although exactly where is not known for certain. So far as we can tell the house mouse was the first to spread into Europe because it was known to the Ancient Greeks. The ship rat seems to have invaded Europe about the 11th or 12th century, nobody can be more exact than that. It was a definite invasion because at certain places in southern Russia there were reports of hordes of rats crossing the rivers at this time. The common or brown rat came later and did not reach the British Isles until the 18th century. The house mouse and the two rodents, by moving into Europe, found their way to what were then the main shipping ports of the world. The first of the rats was the black rat, which found its way on to ships. Later it was ousted by the common rat, except around seaports, which is one reason why it is best to call it the ship rat. In

The common or brown rat that arrived in the British Isles in the eighteenth century

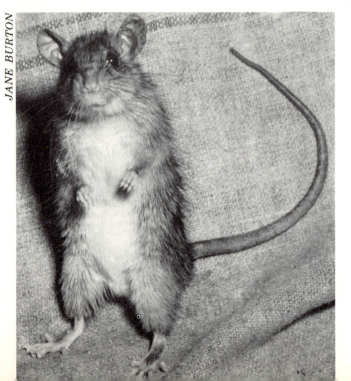

JANE BURTON

time all three rodents have been carried around the world on ships.

Although the spread of these three rodents and the way their fortunes have been linked with those of people makes the most spectacular story of man's commensals, we are left guessing very much as to the time that the spread took place. There is, however, another commensal of man whose spread took place during this century and the story of its spread can be followed almost year by year. The bird is the collared dove. It is in many ways quite an ordinary kind of dove, greyish brown with black feathers in the wings, but we can recognize it best by its black collar bordered with white. We can also recognize it by its monotonous call.

The collared dove was introduced from Asia Minor into south-east Europe in the 18th century, by the Turks, and there it stayed for many years. Then, in 1835, it spread into Bulgaria. It stayed there for quite a long time because the next we hear of it was when it turned up in Belgrade, the capital of Yugoslavia, in 1912. After that the pigeon fairly raced across Europe. It invaded Hungary in 1930, Austria in 1943, Italy in 1944, Germany in 1946, and Holland in 1948. Soon after this there were reports of collared doves seen in England. At first these were disbelieved because the experts thought the birds might have been pet doves that had escaped from aviaries. There were some grounds for this because with aviary birds becoming so popular, there are many escapers; people often see strange birds in the fields or woods, or even in their own

In recent years collared doves have spread from Asia Minor through Europe to Britain

gardens, which later prove to have been aviary escapers. However, in 1955, a pair of collared doves bred in Norfolk and there could no longer be any doubt that the bird had crossed Europe and was now becoming naturalized in the British Isles. In the fifteen years since then, collared doves have spread all over Great Britain, even to the islands off the west of Scotland, and they have also taken up residence in Ireland.

The spread of the collared dove was no accident. The bird's natural food is seeds, although it also eats fruit and berries, and it has taken particularly to cereal grains such as wheat. All along the route across Europe it has been noticed that collared doves are especially liable to take up residence where grain is put down for poultry or at any point where grain is split accidentally: for instance on farms, in warehouses or in railway marshalling yards where grain is being loaded.

Fortunately, the collared dove is not a nuisance in the garden, as is its close relative the wood pigeon, because apart from berries it eats only seeds, whereas the wood pigeon will turn to almost anything that is vegetable. In winter, when the ground is hard with frost or covered with snow, and other foods are short, wood pigeons will eat cabbages almost down to their bare stumps.

The collared dove would not have spread across Europe but for the way man wastes his food. This is probably also true of the house mouse and the two rats as well as some of the others, including insects such as cockroaches and silverfish. (By the way, don't go looking for a fish: the silverfish is a very small wingless insect, with a silvery body shaped like a fish, that scuttles rapidly across the floor when it is disturbed.)

The mouse and the two rats that crossed Europe centuries ago would have been encouraged to do so partly by the spread of agriculture, because all three animals are basically grain eaters. In those days, however, only a small part of the land was cultivated and there were wide stretches of forest

between the patches of arable land. It is highly likely therefore that the rodents were assisted in their emigration by the middens. In those early days every village had its midden, or garbage heap, which was visited by any wild animal searching for food. It has even been suggested that the dog itself first became domesticated through visiting the middens to scavenge. It is interesting to see that foxes are now doing exactly the same thing with our garbage bins and with the litter baskets that are put up all over the countryside to try to keep it tidy. In our parks, after it has snowed, you can often see the footprints of a fox that has gone from one litter basket to another, climbed in, searched among the paper for food and jumped down the other side. In the dead of night you may hear the lid of the garbage bin knocked off, rattling to the ground. It may be a cat that has done it, or it may be a fox. Young scientists have in the past few years gone out at night in large towns to make surveys of how many foxes they see, and from their reports and others it has become fairly clear that the fox is able to settle down even in large towns,

and get a good living from the food we throw away. Exactly the same has happened in North America where the raccoon raids the garbage bins. It does the job more thoroughly than the fox, because it knocks the bin over and scatters the contents all around.

So all these animals are battening on man for food. There is one, however, which as often as not uses our houses for shelter and brings at least some of its own food in with it. This is the yellow-necked mouse which is larger than the house mouse, has a longer tail, and has a yellow or orange patch on its chest or on the sides of its neck. The yellow-necks live out of doors throughout the spring and summer. In autumn they enter houses, often making their home in the upper part of the house. They will help themselves to any fruit or nuts they can find, and they may also raid the larder sometimes for such things as cheese and bacon. But there have been instances in which it is known that yellow-necked mice have carried into the house, and up to the top storey, nuts from trees that were as much as 110 yards from the house.

Control Without Poison

CONSERVATION includes control of pests and also control of pollution. We kill an insect pest with a pesticide and we kill a plant pest with a herbicide. But pesticides and herbicides are usually poisonous chemicals. They find their way into the soil, are washed by rain into streams and rivers, and end up in the sea. All the way they are polluting the soil, the fresh waters and the oceans.

The damage a pesticide can do was shown vividly not long ago when a load of insecticide was spilled into the Rhine, in Germany. In a very short while, thousands of fish were dying all the way down the Rhine to where it enters the sea on the coast of Holland.

Although they can be so damaging, pesticides have their uses provided that they are used wisely, prudently and in reasonable quantities. Everyone agrees, however, that natural control—or biological control, as it is usually called—is better. This is almost a method of "setting a thief to catch a thief". The trouble with biological controls is that they usually require years of research.

Perhaps the best example of a successful biological control is that used on prickly pear in Australia. In its native land, which is North America, the prickly pear is just one of many cacti growing in dry, hot regions. In Mexico it is even put to use, planted around houses as a protective hedge. The pear-shaped fruits of some of the many kinds of prickly pear yield a refreshing juice and the fibres of the trunk were used for making baskets. In 1839, and again in 1860, this cactus was taken to Australia and planted in gardens. Soon new plants began to appear outside the gardens. The prickly pear had gone wild.

Prickly pears have been naturalized and made to serve a useful purpose in southern Europe and north Africa but it was a different story in Australia. Some people say that the prickly pear was taken there as a pot plant, that the owner grew tired of it and threw it on

Prickly pear growing wild in Australia

the rubbish heap, whence pieces of it became scattered and took root. Others say pieces were planted in the hope that its succulent branches would give a watery food for cattle in times of drought.

Whatever the truth, it began to flourish and to spread exceedingly. The spread was especially rapid from 1900 onwards; a quarter of a century later fifty million acres in Queensland and ten million acres in New South Wales were more or less covered with it.

Because the cactus grows anything up to twenty feet high and forms dense thickets of flattened stems and branches, it keeps the ground around it shaded so that no other plants can grow. Since the Australians could find no way of checking its spread, they sent scientists to America to look for its natural enemies. The scientists brought back several kinds of insects, one of which really did the trick. It was a moth named Cactoblastis. Three million of these insects were set free in Australia between 1928 and 1930. The gaudily striped caterpillars greedily ate into the cactus, and in a few years the battle was won. As the miles of prickly pear died to a rotting pulp, the insect began to die out for lack of food. At once the remaining cactus began to spread again, but as soon as this happened the numbers of the insect rose again too. So the balance was restored. Today more than ninety-five per cent of those sixty million acres are free of the cactus and can be cultivated.

The important thing is that nothing other than the prickly pear was damaged and there was no pollution. Moreover the moth, with no natural enemies, remains as a watchdog, ready to increase and spread as soon as the cactus starts to do so.

Cactoblastis moth and its caterpillar feeding on prickly pear

African grey parrots are not only great imitators, but amusing performers also

Bird Mimics

EVERYONE knows that parrots will talk and imitate different kinds of sounds. There are many other birds that will do the same. We always say that they are imitating the sounds without having the least idea of their meaning. So far as parrots are concerned at least this is not quite true. When you study a parrot closely over a number of years you realize that it is using words with about the same intelligence as a child beginning to talk.

Parrots also show a certain amount of skill in what can be best called instrumental music. That is, they are able to use metal or other solid objects to imitate sounds. A simple form of this is when a parrot will imitate a typewriter by banging the top of its beak on a particular piece of metal in its cage which sounds exactly like the particular typewriter that is used within earshot of the bird. In tapping, it also copies the pauses and the hesitations, as well as the speed, which are normal for the person using that typewriter.

Parrots have also been known to imitate a variety of metallic sounds going on around them which they have not heard before. One parrot, for example, went to live in a photographic studio where there were all kinds of metallic clicks from the camera, and metallic sounds from the camera stands being screwed and unscrewed. One day the parrot was seen walking round its cage tapping first one wire and then another until it got the correct imitation of first one metallic sound, then another. When any one of these sounds was repeated the parrot immediately went to the chosen spot and tapped the wire to imitate it. Some of the sounds resembled noises the parrot had already learned to imitate by voice. In that case it would use its voice rather than search for a spot on the wires. So, when the photographer was very busy, with squeaks and clicks coming thick and fast, the parrot would be running round its cage, tapping a wire here, a wire there, making another sound with its voice, and so on.

Another parrot belonged to a lady who owned a very ancient and rickety sewing machine. Her parrot learned to imitate the sound of the sewing machine using both its voice and the wires of its cage. When the bird was alone it would make a perfect imitation, sounding as though someone were sitting at the machine sewing.

No doubt starlings, mynahs, mockingbirds, and that wonderful mimic the lyrebird of Australia, can probably all do as well as the parrots we have been talking about. As a rule they do not have the same opportunities to imitate typewriters or sewing machines.

When a child first learns to speak it not only copies the words it hears, it also copies the actions. Although people had known for many years that birds could imitate sounds, it was always believed that they could not, or would not, imitate actions. Certainly this would be much more difficult for them but there have been a few instances in which it has been seen. Believe it or not, there was one parrot that learned the actions of a man putting on and taking off his coat—or so we are told. There was a starling, also, that learned to imitate the drumming of a woodpecker and to imitate the movement. In the breeding season some woodpeckers drum with their beaks on branches or trunks of trees, nodding their heads like the clapper on an electric bell. This starling not only imitated the sound of the drumming with its voice but also nodded its head rapidly—something a starling never normally does—in imitation of the woodpecker. Another starling is said to have imitated the sound of a handbell, at the same time swaying backwards and forwards in imitation of the movement of the bell. A catbird in the United States learned to call like a kingfisher and at the same time it would fly like a kingfisher.

If anyone doubts these things or thinks them far-fetched he (or she) should watch closely the next time he has the opportunity of studying somebody's pet parrot. He may see the parrot eat an invisible grape. What happens is that when a grape is put in the parrot's food pot, the bird raises its foot to the level of its beak, moving the toes as if grasping something. Then it moves its beak as if chewing, and if you watch closely you may see that it makes movements with its throat as if swallowing. And all this while the grape is lying untouched in the food pot.

Keep Fit Recipe

SINCE a well-grown bull elephant will eat up to 600 pounds of vegetable food a day—that is, about a quarter of a ton—it seems a very small thing to give a zoo elephant a bun. So, you might say, why should there be notices in zoos asking us not to feed the elephants? Behind this question lies a lesson that can be applied to other matters regarding the conservation of our wildlife: do what you are asked to do.

The feeding of all animals by the public, in London Zoo and Whipsnade Park, was banned from January 1, 1968. It had been noticed by the keepers that the elephants had frequent digestive upsets, especially after a bank holiday when the gardens had been crowded with visitors. This was not entirely due to the many different kinds of foods given to the animals, although in fact there were over 900 different kinds—some with the wrappings still on them—during one period of four and a half hours. The main trouble lay elsewhere.

On a day when there were many visitors an elephant would walk out of the Elephant House, where it had spent the night, straight over to where it could hold out its trunk for a titbit. Then it would slowly move round the perimeter of its enclosure, taking food from the people standing there. After that it was likely to be unwell.

Watch was kept after feeding had been prohibited for five months and the movements of one of the elephants were plotted. It walked about, dug at the sand with its foot, threw sand over itself, picked up a log with its trunk and threw it into the air, ran a short distance, walked into its pool, rubbed itself against a wall; in short, it was taking healthy exercise all the time it was not feeding, instead of merely plodding round its enclosure.

JANE BURTON

The Sun by Day, the Stars by Night . . .

IN 1923, Karl von Frisch, an Austrian scientist, discovered that when a honeybee returns to the hive with its load of nectar and pollen it performs a dance on the comb. This may be what he called the round dance or the tail-wagging dance. Von Frisch thought the first meant the bee had found nectar, and that the tail-wagging dance meant it had found pollen. In 1946 he announced to the world that he had been wrong, that the truth was even more remarkable.

In the round dance the bee describes a circle, first making a few turns to the right and then following up with turns to the left, the alternations frequent and regular enough to give the dance a definite character. The more significant tail-wagging dance is by no means so simple. First a bee runs in a half-circle to the right, then back along the diameter to the starting-point; then she describes a similar half-circle to the left. In this way she trips out a figure-of-eight movement, waggling her abdomen a certain number of times during the performance of the complete dance.

The important part of this dance is the straight run along the diameter of

Honeybees performing their round dance (left) and tail-wagging dance (right)

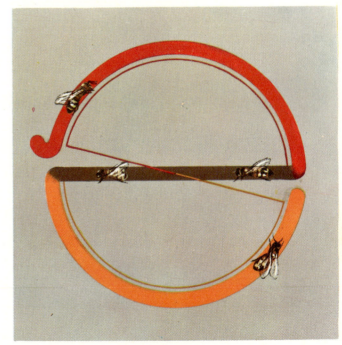

Bees performing their unique dance at the entrance to their hive

the circle. If a bee while dancing moves straight upwards, she is saying that nectar or pollen lies in the direction of the sun; if straight downwards, the direction is opposite to that of the sun. If the movement of the dance makes an angle to the right of the vertical line, then the bees are to seek food at a corresponding angle to the right of the position of the sun. Wherever the food is situated in relation to the position of the sun is reflected by the angle of deviation from the vertical line which the bee makes in its dance.

While we were still marvelling at the way honeybees use the sun—not only to find their way about but to tell other bees what route to take—there came in 1951 the first signs that birds were able

to do the same. Previously it had been a complete mystery how birds on migration, or homing, could find their way so accurately. Now it was becoming clear that they also used the sun. This discovery was not the work of one man. During the years 1946 and 1951, several scientists were working towards the idea, although the main credit must go to Dr. G. V. T. Matthews at Cambridge University and Dr. Gustav Kramer at the Max-Planck Institute in Germany.

Long ago men sailing the seas, or going long journeys overland, must have navigated by the sky, using the sun during the day and the stars by night. We call this celestial navigation. As the years have passed since 1951 it has become more and more clear that

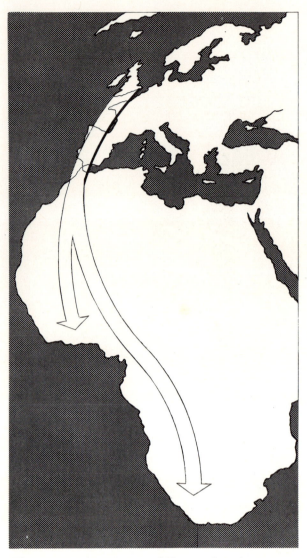

The migration route of the cuckoo in autumn

certain to be using celestial navigation. The first test is to shut out the sky, by blindfolding the animal or putting a blanket of opaque material between it and the sky. Blindfolding is the more usual, and when this is done the animal, instead of going in a straight line, moves about as if lost. When the blinkers are removed it goes straight again.

Another test is to move the animal bodily sideways. For example, the cuckoos in England go due south in autumn to West Africa. If we took one of these, put a ring on its leg, transported it 1,000 miles to the east and released it in eastern Europe, it would still fly due south but would end up in East Africa.

One set of experiments was made on fishes that fed around a coral reef by day but swam on a south-westerly course to an undersea cave for the night. First, experiments were made with blindfolding the fish. Then, some of them were netted, marked and carried carefully and still very much alive several miles to the south. There they were released and as evening drew on they set course to the southwest only to reach a destination as many miles south of their usual cave as they had been taken south from their feeding grounds.

Young salmon go down to the sea, where they spend several years feeding and growing. Their feeding grounds may be as much as 600 miles from the mouth of the river in which they were hatched. Then comes the urge to spawn. The salmon heads back to the land, finds the mouth of the river it came from, and swims up the river to the self-

many animals other than honeybees and birds find their way by celestial navigation. The techniques and the know-how used by von Frisch, Matthews and Kramer have been used by other scientists studying frogs and toads, fishes and other animals. For some of these animals it is even now only suspected that they use celestial navigation. The full proof has yet to be obtained. We do, however, have proof for some, and the suspicion for others amounts almost to a certainty.

Basically the tests are simple. If an animal is in the habit of travelling from one place to another over a longish distance, so that it cannot see its destination or even see landmarks, it is almost

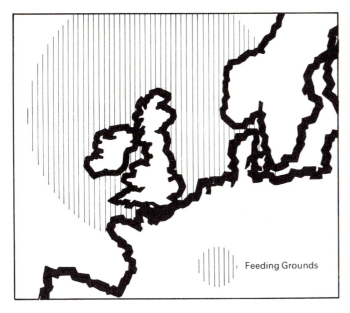 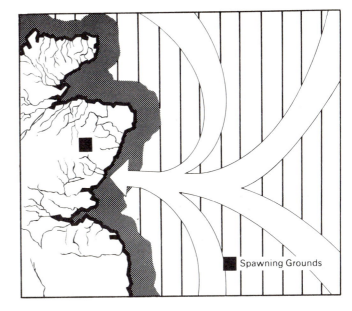

Feeding grounds of salmon (left) and their migration routes (right)

same stream in which it hatched.

It has been suspected for at least a hundred years that the salmon could recognize by smell the water from its own little stream where it was hatched. Since this water mingles with that from other tributaries its odour must be very diluted when it finally empties into the sea, there to become even more diluted by the sea-water. For a salmon to pick up the smell at the river mouth is remarkable enough. For it to be able to pick it up after the water from the stream has travelled anything up to 600 miles in the ocean water, becoming more and more dispersed, must be well-nigh impossible.

For the last fifty years or more scientists have puzzled over this. Now, tests carried out on Pacific salmon leave little doubt that the fish, when their time comes, head for approximately the right place on the coast, using celestial navigation. Once near the river mouth they start nosing about until they pick up the smell of the water from the stream in which they were hatched.

A salmon leap where salmon, going upstream to spawn, can even overcome such obstacles as weirs

HUGH SIBLEY

Mother koala with her baby on her back at home among the Australian eucalyptus trees

Australia's
Most Endearing Animal

THE KOALA is probably the best known of all Australian animals after the kangaroo. It has been called affectionately the Australian Teddy Bear. It is bear-like, about two feet high, with tufted ears and a prominent beak-like snout and no tail, and it lives in the eucalyptus trees. Even those who have never been to Australia must be familiar with this charming animal, especially from photographs of the mother koala up in a tree, with her baby riding pick-a-back and almost as big as she is.

In spite of the koala's gentle disposition and delightful appearance, the hand of the fur trader has been heavy upon it. In one year alone, in 1924, over two million koala skins were exported from Australia. At one time the koala lived in Western and South Australia, as well as in the south east of the continent, but by the 1930's it had been wiped out except for a small number that continued to survive in south-eastern Australia.

This drastic loss in numbers was not

entirely due to the koala being killed off for its fur. It is what we call a specialist feeder. Most animals will change their diet from season to season, and usually, if driven to it by famine, an animal will make do with something other than its usual food. Not so the koala. It seldom eats anything other than the leaves of the eucalyptus, and these gum trees (as the eucalyptus are called) are steadily being felled as the country is opened up for farming.

Only a few years ago there was real fear for the survival of the koala, for it certainly seemed to be in danger of vanishing from the face of the earth. Happily it has been saved by public interest, which ensured not only that fewer of them were killed, but also that reserves or natural parks containing eucalyptus were set aside specially for their use. The moment this animal is protected it begins to increase in numbers. For example, a few koalas were placed in sanctuary among the eucalyptus trees on French Island early in this century. Within a few years they had increased in numbers so much that they were eating out the supply of trees and so were in danger of starvation. Some of them had to be taken to other islands and also on to the mainland to prevent this.

Another thing that has helped the koala is the study that has been made of the way it lives, including the way it eats and what it eats. There were two surprises that came out of these studies, the first concerning its food and the other about its drinking. As to its food, it used to be thought not only that the koala would eat the leaves from one particular kind of eucalyptus, but also that it would eat only certain leaves from these particular trees. What we now know is that its diet is not so restricted as this, that koalas will eat the leaves of several species of eucalyptus and will sometimes eat the leaves from other entirely different trees.

The name "koala" was originally given to the animal by the Australian Aborigines and it is said to mean "no water", because the koala was believed never to drink. This seemed very likely because they spend so much time in the trees, and when they do come down to the ground it is usually only to go from one tree to a fresh one. When the Australian scientists really came to study the koala, however, they found that it will quite readily swim across rivers, and when it comes out of the water on the other side it licks its fur and swallows the water. It has also been seen to drink from pools of water after heavy rain.

Eucalyptus leaves are a koala's staple diet

When Pigeon Slaves Were Freed

IN ANY big town in Britain or in continental Europe, as well as in other parts of the world, you will find pigeons. You will find them especially where there are large buildings, and in London the pigeons of Trafalgar Square have become a tourist attraction. Some people like to see them and enjoy feeding them. Other people dislike them because their droppings soil the walls of buildings and because—they say—pigeons carry disease.

Have you ever stopped to wonder where these pigeons came from and why they are there? Mankind has been using pigeons for two thousand years or more, as messengers. He has also used them for fresh meat, keeping them in what are called pigeon houses, or dovecotes.

The pigeon chosen for domestication, as messengers, racing pigeons, pets and for food, all came from one species, the rock dove. The native home of the rock dove was, and still is, on cliffs and in rocky gorges all over Europe, Asia and parts of northern Africa. For the descendants of the rock dove, the feral pigeons of today, large buildings are man-made cliffs. Window-sills and parapets are the equivalent of the rocky cliff ledges on which their ancestors used to perch and nest. These pigeons are called "feral" because this word denotes an animal that has been domesticated, and then has gone wild and continued to breed in a wild state.

To get some idea of how many pigeons used to be kept for the use of one household, let me take you to a pigeon house just beyond my boundary fence. It looks like a ruined tower, an octagonal red brick building of the mid-16th century. At one time it had a wooden roof and inside, at the centre, was a heavy pole reaching to the roof, fixed so that it could be easily made to revolve. The inside wall is built to form a regular series of cavities from ground level to the top of the tower, each one large enough for a pair of pigeons to roost and nest in. Each cavity has a sill of ironstone below its entrance, for the pigeons to land on. There are 300 cavities, room enough for 600 pigeons to nest. Since the usual brood is two there could have been at any one time 1,200 pigeons, including parents and young. When the pigeon house was in use there would be one or more arms to the central pole, against which a ladder could be leaned. So a man, by turning the pole and moving his ladder round, would be able to put his hand in turn into each of the cavities in the wall.

You may well be wondering how I know that this pigeon house was built in the mid-16th century. The answer lies in the size of the bricks. Had it been

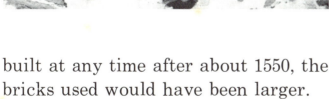

JANE BURTON

Above: London pigeon on the railings of St. James's Park. Left: sixteenth century pigeon house and its interior, showing nesting holes

built at any time after about 1550, the bricks used would have been larger.

In the 16th century the house of the local lord of the manor stood near where the pigeon house now stands. In it would have been the owner, his family and his servants. There were no roads then. The nearest town was five miles away, with no butcher's shop nearer than that. Pigeons breed almost all the year round, especially when they are domesticated. So, when the countryside was covered with snow or everywhere was muddy because of heavy rain,

nobody need go short of food. There were always pigeon eggs or pigeon pie.

As the centuries passed and roads were built and shops became more numerous, the need for these pigeon houses grew less and less. Nobody troubled to repair them and they fell into ruin. Here and there a few still remain, some in better condition than the one described here. For the most part, however, they have disappeared. The pigeons found their way into towns, where every large building became a large pigeon house, or artificial cliff, whichever way you like to think of it. The descendants of the inmantes of the pigeon houses and dovecotes are the feral pigeons of today.

Jelly for Tea

SOMETIMES a jellyfish gets stranded by the tide. We look at it with curiosity. Perhaps we turn it over to look at the other side. Usually we look around for a piece of stick to do this, or we use the toe of our shoe, because we have been told jellyfishes sting, as indeed they do. Some can sting so badly that people have died of the stings, but these venomous jellyfishes are found mainly in tropical seas. Many bathers swimming among a shoal of ordinary jellyfishes have come back to the shore with red weals on their bodies, as if they had fallen among nettles.

The stings are from thousands of tiny stinging cells (sometimes called nettle cells because they sting like nettles) in the tentacles, used by the jellyfish to paralyse its prey. However, dangerous though a jellyfish may be in the sea, it is soon harmless on land, especially under a hot sun. Before the tide has come in again a stranded jellyfish is little more than a pale patch of moisture on the sand.

You would think there could be little nourishment in an animal that is about ninety-five per cent water, and little joy in eating one with so many stings. Yet many animals do eat them and there are some animals that consume them in large numbers. Several seabirds eat jellyfishes and the frigate-birds, or man-o'-war birds, eat lots of them. Frigate-birds have been called the feathered buccaneers of the tropic seas. They spend most of their time over water, coming to land only to nest, and they chase any seabird with a fish in its bill until it drops it, when the frigate-bird swoops and catches it. Frigate-birds also catch their own food, snatching it from the water, including jellyfishes.

The hawksbill turtle and the logger-head turtle also eat quantities of jelly-fishes, often getting stung all round their eyes in the process, and so does that most curious of fishes, the ocean sunfish. This is almost circular in out-line, like a huge plate of living flesh, up to eleven feet across, without a tail and with only small fins. It is an absurd looking fish with a small mouth and small eyes. It weighs nearly a ton fully grown, yet has a tiny brain and a spinal cord only an inch long.

Until the days of skin-diving the only sunfishes seen were floating idly at the surface on their flat side, as if basking in the sun. Now we know they are very different below the surface, swimming upright, and that those seen at the sur-face are dying.

If this huge fish, with a huge body to keep up, can live on jellyfishes there must be something good in them. The people of the Philippines think so, for jellyfishes pickled in vinegar are sold in their markets. In Japan, also, people preserve them in a mixture of alum and salt between steamed leaves of a kind of oak. They then soak the whole in water and serve it with condiments. Somebody writing in 1758 tells us jellyfishes were sometimes eaten in Cornwall.

Now, this is where we have to be careful. There may be more in this than meets the eye, especially so far as the frigate-birds, turtles and sunfishes are concerned. Several kinds of fishes, when young, shelter under the jellyfishes, protected from enemies by the stinging tentacles. They leave the shelter of their jellyfish guardian to feed but dash under cover the moment they are dis-turbed, such as when a frigate-bird swoops down or a turtle or sunfish come near. Perhaps these animals are not merely eating jelly, but fish as well—something much nearer the highly nutritious jellied eels!

The ocean sunfish (left) and turtle (right)

Dressing Up

THERE is a story from the early days of the colonization of Canada which runs like this. A British general met an Indian chief for a pow-pow, in the depths of winter. The general was muffled up in layers of warm clothing so that only his face was exposed to the weather. The Red Indian merely had a blanket thrown round his shoulders. The general asked the chief how he could stand the cold with his body exposed. The chief pointed out that the general's face was open to the weather. "Yes," replied the general, "but my face is used to it." The chief is said to have answered "Me all face."

Chimpanzees are game for anything . . .

G. A. DUNCAN

It is not only the North American Indians that could stand up to cold weather almost unclothed. The people of Tierra del Fuego, at the other end of the Americas, were equally hardy. This makes one wonder why mankind took to wearing clothes in the first place, especially as the human race seems to have originated in East Africa.

Young gorillas and chimpanzees in zoos are fond of draping straw, newspapers or sacking around their shoulders. Also, there are many stories of these apes and of pet monkeys putting pots and bowls on their heads, wearing them like hats. Apes, especially, and monkeys are our nearest relatives and they behave very like us in many ways. One of these ways seems to be a love of dressing up. Our earliest forefathers went about naked and ate mainly fruit and vegetables. Then they learned how to hunt and kill large animals and to skin them, to eat their flesh. Did they look at these skins and think what excellent coverings they would make for their bodies? Or did some of them, like young gorillas and chimpanzees, drape the skins around their shoulders for fun, and only then discover that they kept out the cold?

We shall never know the answers to these questions. What we do know is that as soon as Early Man had learned how to make weapons, such as bows and arrows and flint-tipped spears, he hunted animals for food. He also killed the dangerous ones in self-defence. Then, when he had found how useful their skins could be, he started killing animals that were harmless, or useless for food, but carried a good fur coat.

So long as the human race was small in number this mattered little. But as the numbers of people increased, so the numbers they killed went up by leaps and bounds; and this has been going on increasingly ever since. Many large animals that became extinct half a million years ago were once thought to have died out naturally. We now have reason to believe they were killed off by men, in what is now spoken of as man's over-kill; that is, killing for protection, for food and for other reasons, but doing so in excess of actual needs.

One of the first fur-bearing animals to feel the brunt of this attack, at least in historic times, was the beaver. It was wiped out in England as early as Anglo-Saxon times and by the 12th century it survived in two places only, one in Wales and one in Scotland. In continental Europe it was much the same story except that there are a few places, as in the River Rhône in France, where it still lives under protection. The beaver in the United States and Canada was going the same way, but in Canada it was conserved. In order to increase its numbers live beavers were caught, transported by plane and released into rivers where beavers used to live but had been wiped out.

Another fur-bearer that suffered badly was the chinchilla. Its soft silky fur, with more hairs to the square inch

Beavers, once quite a common sight, are now only surviving where they are protected in several parts of the world, and in the United States and Canada, they are being re-introduced to rivers where they had been completely wiped out by man

than the fur of any other known animal, became fashionable for making women's coats. The chinchilla, which lives in the Andes of Peru, is the size of a smallish rabbit, so it is easy to imagine how many chinchillas had to be killed and skinned to make even one fur coat. But these coats fetched high prices, so it paid hunters to go to Peru and go up into the mountains to kill as many chinchillas as they could find. In a very short while the chinchilla was on the verge of extinction, so the Peruvian government passed laws forbidding the export of this animal and its skins.

It happened, however, that somebody had caught some chinchillas alive and had taken them to the United States and started to breed them. This idea caught on and at one time a breeding pair fetched £300. Then chinchilla fur went out of fashion and nowadays a breeding

R. W. VAUGHAN

M. F. SOPER

The southern (left) and New Zealand (right) fur seals—both highly valued for their skins

pair of these animals can be bought for as little as £5.

About this same time as the fashion in chinchilla fur there came a craze for ladies' shoes and handbags made in snake skin, and large numbers of snakes were killed. This was followed by a fashion for these same articles in crocodile skin. Crocodiles are more easily killed than snakes. You have only to go to a river in the tropics, wait for the crocodile to surface or walk ashore and then shoot it. There was such a demand for crocodile skins that these reptiles looked like being wiped out almost everywhere in the world. It was even said that crocodiles had at one time grown so scarce in some places, and the price of the skin had risen so high, that it paid a man to charter a plane to go and shoot even a small crocodile.

The world's seals would have gone the same way as the crocodile had not some scientists rebelled at the way they were being killed. Today, most species of fur seals are being properly conserved, and the way this is being done shows that it is possible to take a harvest from an animal species without wiping it out.

Killing for protection can be justified and so can killing for food, but killing for fashion is without virtue. Several species of birds, notably the egret, were almost wiped out because women wanted the hats decorated with their plumes. So mad were people to make money out of egrets' plumes, and in such a hurry to do so, that those who trapped the egrets would chop off their plumes while the birds were still alive. Fashion is apt to lead to excesses of this kind.

We are now seeing a new turn in the killing of animals for their skins. It is fashionable today to have a coat made of the skin of tigers, leopards or cheetahs as well as of the rarer cats such as the clouded leopard. Unless there is a change for the better these Big Cats, already much reduced in numbers, may be in danger of disappearing for ever.

True, these animals are wild beasts, powerful and at times ferocious, and they can be a danger to human life. Yet they have a value in the balance of nature. It is known that when, for instance, the leopards in any district are killed off, other animals that ravage crops increase in numbers and become a pest. In India this means the deer, in Africa the baboons. Farmers in Africa have spoken of having a leopard living on the farm, which gave no trouble but kept down the small animals that destroyed the crops.

Upset Nature in this and in other ways, and she has a way of hitting back, unless what we do is based on sound knowledge. In Britain we have a problem of this kind at the moment. The mink, a relative of the weasel but larger, has a fine fur, valued for making women's coats. At first wild mink were trapped for the fur market. Then some were caught alive and farmed; live American mink were farmed in Britain. Occasionally they escaped, then the escapees began to breed. Today there are feral mink—that is, escaped mink gone wild—that are breeding and spreading along the river banks. They are good swimmers. They feed on fish,

A feral mink keeps a sharp look-out for any unsuspecting fish

JANE BURTON

A young Nile crocodile partly submerged

and they also kill birds, including poultry, so the angler is upset and also the poultry farmer. At the moment the feral mink are more a local nuisance than anything else, but in the years ahead they may become an acute problem—and all because of fashion!

As to the larger "killers" such as the tiger, it is of interest to note that in the Sunderbans, an area of mangrove swamps and jungle in East Pakistan, the tigers have become man-eaters. Men going into the jungle to fetch wood or gather wild honey do so at their own risk. Even fishermen are in danger from a tiger swimming to the boat. In past times everyone's first thought would have been to organize a hunt to go out and shoot some of the tigers. However, times are changing. Today, the first thing to happen is that somebody has asked why the tigers should have be-become dangerous. Perhaps it is because the deer they usually feed on have become scarce? The next step, and this has been taken at the suggestion of the International Union for the Conservation of Nature, has been that

the Pakistan government has set aside two areas of the Sunderbans as nature reserves, in which nobody may go except the game wardens and scientists. Having thus done all they can to protect human life as well as the tigers, the government will set in motion a research programme to find out why the tigers have suddenly become so dangerous.

The cause may not be a shortage of food, if we are to judge from what we know of the crocodiles in Africa. There it is well known that in some places the crocodiles are dangerous to people, while in other places they seem to be quite harmless. Nobody can be sure why this is so. At any rate, there are some people who think crocodiles are worth preserving. The Game and Fish Preservation Board of the Natal Parks have a crocodile rearing project in Zululand where crocodile eggs are hatched and the young protected and reared. When well enough grown these crocodiles are used to re-stock rivers from which crocodiles have dis-appeared.

The Spreading Chestnut Tree

IN MY garden is a ring of horse chestnut trees, each fifty to sixty feet high, the diameter of the ring being about forty yards. There used to be thirty of these trees but five of them have fallen.

The horse chestnut is unlike the true or sweet chestnut in almost every way except that its nuts are also enclosed in a prickly husk. Its native home seems to have been Greece but in the early 16th century, or possibly even before that, it became a fashionable tree to plant in gardens. Today it is growing in all parts of Europe and western Asia and even in North America. The ring in my garden came from a single tree planted there about 1750, and the trees now standing are all from branches that layered themselves.

About half a mile from my house is another well-grown horse chestnut. When I came to live here twelve years ago its lower branches curved down towards the ground. Today some of these have not only touched the ground, they have become partly buried at that point and have there started to throw out roots. In other places I have seen horse chestnuts with only one or two branches that have curved down, touched the ground and rooted, and the outer half of the branch is beginning to grow straight up to form a new trunk.

The original horse chestnut in my garden died of extreme old age about fifty years ago but thirty of its branches had already layered and thrown up fresh trunks. The parent tree was over 250 years old when it finally rotted away. Whenever one of the new trunks has fallen I have had it sawn across near the base to count the rings and these have numbered between 120 and 150. So at some time in the 19th century, when the parent tree was already 200 years old, its lower branches drooped to the ground and the outer half of each grew up to form the new trunks. What is more, the inner part of some of the branches, now very much thickened, can be seen lying along the ground still joined to the bases of the new trunks.

A branch of the original horse chestnut lying along the ground, still joined to the base of the tree that grew up from it

ROBERT BURTON

Black/White Moths

THE PEPPERED moth has been much in the scientific news in recent years. The females are about two and a quarter inches across the wings, and the males are smaller. Centuries ago peppered moths had white wings peppered with black spots. During the day they rested on tree trunks with their wings flattened against the bark, and in this position were very hard to see. As a result birds searching for insects mostly overlooked these moths, although at night when the moths were on the wing some were caught by bats. Even so, the peppered moths enjoyed a fair

measure of safety because they looked so much like the lichens growing on the bark.

Every so often one or more of the moths from a brood would be black (or melanic, as it is called, from the Greek word meaning black). These showed up against the grey lichens and insect-eating birds soon picked them off.

Then came the Industrial Revolution. Trees in towns became black with soot from factory chimneys and from the chimneys of the crowded streets that sprang up around the factories. Now it was the turn of the melanic moths to enjoy an advantage. Their black wings matched the soot-covered bark and the birds overlooked them, but they could easily see the white, more normal variety, and picked them off. So, from the peppered moth being white with black spots and only rarely black, it became black and only rarely white, except of course in places like the north of Scotland which are not industrial.

For many years scientists have studied these and many other moths. They have found about seventy different kinds of moths that have changed to black, and for the same reason. This changing to black because of the soot is known as industrial melanism.

Since 1952 the control of smoke, giving smokeless zones, has led to a marked reduction of soot in the air. Our towns are getting cleaner. The lichens, killed off by the soot, are again growing on the trees. Even town buildings, on the walls of which moths often settle, have been cleaned of their soot. Scientists were interested to know what was happening to the moths, so they went back and studied them. What they have found is that the white and black-spotted moth of the days before the Industrial Revolution is gradually coming back and the melanic moths are becoming rarer. It may take a few more years of "clean" cities before the position is completely restored, but at least it is now well on the way.

Peppered moths blending and contrasting with the bark of tree trunks

Treadmills for Pets

PEOPLE sometimes buy a cage for a hamster, or for tame mice, and find it has a wheel in it for the animal to run in. They take it home, put their pet inside, and watch it run in the wheel for long spells at a time, then come out from the wheel and lie apparently exhausted on the bottom of the cage. They then ask whether it is bad for an animal to have this wheel. The answer can be seen in the story of the elephant at the London Zoo on page 23.

It has long been the practice to give caged animals an exercise wheel. At first the wheel was put in when it was popular to keep squirrels in cages, as pets. Then a wheel was put in for tame mice, and now hamsters. There is nothing to show that any pet has died as a result. Rather, there is every reason to believe it improves their health. Certainly, it prevents their being bored. Indeed, small animals put in cages will often run round and round, as if in an imaginary wheel.

I had a tame stoat once. Although it was let out into the house, with all outer doors and windows closed, it had to be put in a cage at other times. Stoats are likely to kill birds and some of our neighbours kept poultry. While in the cage, and especially at night, the stoat would dash round its cage in circles, not just on the floor, but around the walls, using them as a wheel; but instead of a wheel going round and the

This gull in Whipsnade Park spent much of its time playing with an old tennis ball

animal remaining stationary, in this way the animal was moving and its "wheel" stayed still. The stoat would run in circles in this way at high speed for several minutes on end, then lie down and sleep.

One of the big changes made in zoos in the last half century springs from the realization that boredom can be as bad for animals as for human beings. They need something to play with, something to keep them on the move. In the wild most of an animal's waking hours are spent on the move, searching for food. In captivity its food is provided so it needs something else to keep it on the move, and this is provided by play.

It is not many years since some scientists—those studying animal behaviour—were against the idea that animals play in the same sense that we play. Today this view is changing. This thing we call play is to be seen particularly in animals in captivity, or in domesticated animals which have food supplied to them. For example, there was a gull in Whipsnade Park that spent much of its time on a rockery with an old tennis ball. It would push the ball with its beak from the top of the rockery so that it ran down to the bottom. The gull would follow it and, once the ball had reached the bottom of the rockery, would laboriously push it up again to the top with its beak and then nudge it so that it rolled down again. It probably enjoyed this as much as someone laboriously pulling a sledge to the top of a slope in order to have the brief pleasure of sliding down on it.

Saved by Fire

ONE OF the worst things anyone can do after a picnic is go away leaving the remains of a fire. It may set the grass on fire or, in a wood, set the bushes and trees ablaze. Those who have been near a heath or forest fire will know how terrifying it can be. Yet in one part of the world setting a forest on fire is the only way of saving one species of bird from becoming extinct.

This place, a small part of the State of Michigan in the United States, only 100 miles by 80 miles, is the home of Kirtland's warbler. This is a small song-bird about the size of a house sparrow, olive-green on the head and back and with a pale yellow breast. There are many kinds of warblers in different parts of the world. All are small and none is brightly coloured, although all sing sweetly which is how they get their name.

Kirtland's warbler is not found over the whole of this area, only where there are stands of Jack pine, and even then only where the pines have been burnt several years before. In fact, there are only about a thousand of them, all told. This small bird, which feeds on insects, cannot prosper except where the pines are not less than five feet and not more than fifteen feet tall. Moreover, there must be no thick bushes or shrubs under the trees. These usually grow in plantations before the young trees grow to five feet or more and smother them, or after the pines have grown tall enough to let in the light.

At first it was puzzling to see why this warbler should nest only in this small area of the northern United States, between Lake Michigan and Lake Huron, since there are forests of Jack pine in many other parts of the country. Then it was found that the bird nests in little tunnels in the ground, and the soil must be light and sandy if it is to be able to dig the tunnels. The soil must also be well drained if the nests are not to be flooded during heavy rains. In Michigan the conditions are ideal.

Now comes the question, why should this little bird be so fastidious about the height of the trees among which it lives? The answer seems to be that in plantations of young pines, with ground beneath them more or less bare of shrubs or of plants other than mosses, grasses or small herbs, there are few animals other than small birds and insects. This means enemies are few, and the need to avoid enemies seems to be borne out by the behaviour of Kirtland's warbler in winter.

At the end of summer all the birds fly to the Bahamas, the islands to the east of Florida. There they settle only on the driest and most barren ground, where enemies are likely to be few.

Another advantage of fire among the Jack pines is that the heat makes the cones pop open, releasing their seeds several years before they would otherwise do so. These fall on ground covered with ash which makes the seedling trees grow more quickly. This has a special importance in view of what we have to say next.

Forest fires caused by careless people occur frequently, so in the past there was always plenty of burnt forest to give the right size of pines. Before that, in prehistoric times, there was lightning and other natural causes to set the forest ablaze. In these modern times, with more people getting out into the country there are even more fires. At the same time our fire-fighting equipment and methods are better, and usually the fires are put out very quickly. There were fears therefore that perhaps Kirtland's warbler might not have enough suitable habitat.

In 1963, 4,000 acres of the Huron National Forest were set aside as a management area for the warbler. In the spring of 1964, before the warblers had returned north from the Bahamas, 500 of these acres were deliberately burned, on a still day and with all kinds of fire-fighting equipment such as water pumps, bulldozers and helicopters standing by to make sure only the 500 acres were burned. The idea was to follow this with other burnings in future years, so that Kirtland's warbler would always have suitable forests in which to nest.

A male Kirtland's warbler, for whose preservation forests are set on fire, leaves its nest in a tunnel in the ground

RON AUSTING

Big Cats in the Cold

THE LION has long been acclaimed the king of beasts, the one animal to combine great courage and strength with generosity and mercy towards its vanquished foes. The early kings of England liked to think they had these same qualities, and adopted the lion as their emblem. In more recent times we have talked about the British Lion as a national symbol. Now we actually have lions living in our countryside—in parks it is true, and fenced in—in Longleat Park and the Windsor Safari Park.

Knowing what our climate is like, often very cold in winter, it seems strange that lions can flourish so well in England. Yet there used to be lions in England in prehistoric times. Because their fossils are found in caves we speak of the cave lion, but in fact this lion differed little from the lions of today, and some people think the two belong to the same species, *Felis leo*. Long ago there were lions over much of Europe too; in Ancient Greece there were still lions living wild in the fourth century B.C., according to the historians of the time.

There were lions in Asia Minor, just across from Greece, even later than that time, and from Asia Minor to India lions survived until the last few centuries. Today, the only lions in Asia are in a reserve in India, in the Gir forest, at Kathiawar. There are only a few hundred of them, and they are not fenced in. People live in the Gir forest and their cattle are sometimes killed by the lions, and every year some people are killed too. Because these are the last of the Asiatic lions, however, they are protected. Throughout the rest of southern Asia, as in Europe, man has killed off the lion because it was a danger to human life.

The story is only slightly different for Africa. There used to be lions from North Africa to the Cape. The northern lion, the Barbary lion, and the southern one, the Cape lion, have been killed off. Elsewhere in Africa lions are much fewer than they used to be and now live mainly in reserves and national parks.

A lion in a lazy mood

JANE BURTON

All this explains why, since the early years of this century, we have grown used to the idea that the lion is a dweller in hot countries. So we are surprised to see the lions of Longleat and Windsor wandering about in snow in winter, and even rolling in it and seeming to enjoy it. This is merely one more example of how readily some animals, especially warm-blooded animals, can adapt to a change of habitat and even to changes in climate. But as we have seen with birds, everything depends on proper care and, more important, on correct food.

Lions living in northern climates, in zoos and parks, have a thicker layer of fat than those living in tropical climates. Because of this layer of fat their hair is sleeker and grows longer. The animals look in good condition and the extra fat and the longer hair keep them warm. All that is then needed is a good shelter without draughts and a good bed of straw. In fact, the house mouse years ago pointed the way to what can happen. Some house mice took to living in cold meat stores. They grew longer coats and were quite happy—even though it was perpetual winter for them.

This does not mean you can take any tropical animal and set it loose in a temperate climate. For one thing, it must be acclimatized; that is, it must be allowed to get used to low temperatures by slow degrees. After that, as we have seen, the correct food (which usually means a richer food than normal) and a good shelter carry them along. But not all tropical warm-blooded animals can be acclimatized to northern countries. The marmosets of South America need to be kept in heated rooms. So do hummingbirds, because they are peculiar in going each

Five lions enjoying their comfortable life at Longleat

A. CHRISTIE

Manchurian tiger

Bengal tiger

The migration route of the tiger

and Indonesia. Even today, after many centuries, the southern tigers cannot stand the heat of a tropical day and must lie either in the shade or in a stream to keep cool.

There ought really to be little surprise in seeing the Longleat and Windsor lions playing in the snow. Zoos in temperate latitudes have long had such things as ostriches from hot Africa, emus from Australia, cockatoos, sun bears, camels, flamingoes, ibises and other hot climate animals in the open in winter. The keepers at Amsterdam Zoo believe that fresh air is one of the most important needs of these animals. Experience shows that animals kept in heated rooms in zoos are often not in such good condition as their fellows that have been acclimatized and then kept in the open. Moreover, the Ontario Zoo, in southern Canada, has had lions and tigers out in the open in winter in thirty-six degrees of frost.

Even in Ontario the cold can be such that the slightest breeze seems to cut your face like a knife. Farther north, in the bitter winter winds of the Alberta Game Farm, there are African and Indian antelopes and zebras not only acclimatized and living happily but even breeding in winter. They can stand up to the driving winds and the snow because as well as growing longer coats, they have richer food and good shelters with plenty of straw for beds. All the same, the idea of zebras living in Canada in the depth of winter does seem a little odd. It certainly goes to show what can be done in taking animals from one part of the world to another in order to preserve the species.

night into a sort of semi-hibernation. In most warm-blooded animals the body temperature drops five to ten degrees, but in hummingbirds it goes down to almost that of the surrounding air. Hummingbirds taken to temperate countries and left out in cold weather would simply go to sleep and not wake up again.

Tigers do well in northern zoos. The famous Bengal tiger, Suleika, had twenty-six cubs in the Amsterdam zoo, the last when she was seventeen years old. But tigers are really cold country animals. They started in Siberia long ago, then spread southwards to India

Not many lions have the chance to play in snow that these do . . .

From Any Angle . . .

Here are some slightly odd views of quite ordinary natural scenes or objects. How many of them can you identify?

ALL PHOTOGRAPHS BY JANE BURTON

7

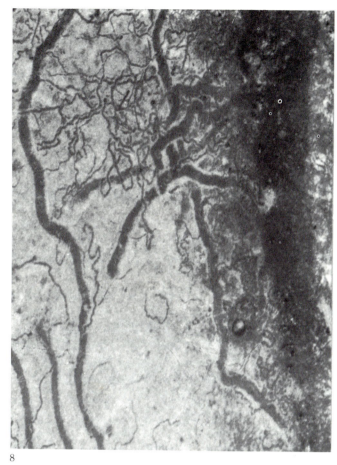

8

Now read the explanations below and find out how observant you are.

1. *This is not a sea-anemone. It is a toadstool, viewed from above. The clue lies at the left of the picture, where part of another similar toadstool can be seen from the side, showing some of the spore-bearing gills.*

2. *Not a colony of butterflies, but a cluster of ships' barnacles. Although these look like molluscs they are, in fact, crustaceans— relatives of the crab.*

3. *Fountains of water—but what caused them? The answer is coot. When coot are attacked by a bird of prey, they sit on their tails on the water and splash with their feet, so setting up this kind of water-barrage. It may well be the earliest form of defence against air attack.*

4. *It might have been a caterpillar's back, but it is, in fact, the underside of a frond of hart's tongue fern. If you look closely you will see that the black stripes are actually*

groups of spore capsules.

5. *Not strange growths on rocks, but hazelnuts. A nuthatch will jam these into crevices in the bark of a tree to hold them firm while it breaks them open with its bill.*

6. *You probably guessed a sea-creature, but did you know it was an octopus? Threatened by an enemy, it has thrown its skin into goose-pimples in an attempt to disguise itself as a lump of rock. It has even contracted its eye so as not to give the game away.*

7. *This one may look more like an octopus than the last, but it is, in fact, a frond of bracken beginning to unfold in early spring.*

8. *Worms? No, these are the tracks left by winkles of various sizes, walking across the sand. The winkle's single flat-soled foot contracts to push it forward and in so doing digs into the sand, so that the winkle leaves a lightly-scored trail wherever it goes.*

A large black hunting wasp drags away a baboon spider that it has paralysed

Tool-Users

THERE must have been a time when man lived by gathering food daily, just as animals do. In South-East Asia even today there is one tribe that does exactly that, walking through the forests picking berries, catching insects and eating small things of that kind. There came a time, however, when man learned to use tools. At first he shaped pieces of wood and later bones and flints, and from these simple beginnings has developed the tremendous technology we have today. So we have come to speak of Man the Toolmaker, and a century ago, or even less, it was usual to say that we are the only species that uses tools. To a large extent this is still true, but there have been a number of surprises.

We now know that one of the bower-birds of Australia not only builds a bower of sticks and decorates it with shells, flowers and feathers, but also paints the inside of the bower with the brightly coloured juices of berries. What is more, this bird uses a piece of stick as a sort of paint brush. Then somebody noticed that a hunting wasp uses a tool. Hunting wasps are small insects that dig tunnels in sandy ground, the females placing in these caterpillars that they have stung and paralysed. In each tunnel an egg is laid and the grub hatching from it eats the caterpillar. The female of one of these hunting wasps closes the entrance to the burrow with sand and then picks up in her jaws a sand grain larger than the others and with it hammers down the sand blocking the entrance.

In the Galapagos Islands off the Pacific coast of tropical America, are a number of birds known as Darwin's finches. One of these will break off a thorn or a cactus spine, hold it in its beak and use it to probe the crevices in bark for insect grubs. When it has levered out a grub, the bird drops the thorn, eats the grub, and then picks the thorn up again to go on using it.

A chimpanzee will take a twig and poke it into the tiny holes in a termites' nest. This causes the insects to attack the twig, whereupon the chimpanzee pulls it out, eats the termites clinging to it and then has another go. Chimpanzees have also been seen to throw sticks at an enemy, and a female elephant will sometimes pull up a sapling to beat her calf. These are all things that our earliest ancestors probably did before they learned to make proper tools.

It is true that even if we put all these things together they do not amount to a row of beans compared with the way man makes and uses tools today, but the interesting part of the story is that in almost all of these instances the person who first reported having seen the animal using a tool was disbelieved. For example, off the Pacific coast of North America lives the sea otter. About forty years ago an American scientist claimed that she had seen a sea otter dive to the bottom of the sea and come up holding a clam and a flat stone. She said the otter turned on its back, placed the stone on its chest, held the clam between its front paws and brought it down with a bang on the stone and cracked it. The scientist made drawings of what she had seen, but many of her fellow scientists shook their heads in disbelief. There was no reason why they should have done so because after all a sea otter was merely doing something very like what the song thrush will do when it uses a flat stone, known as its "anvil", to break the shells of snails it wants to eat.

Another surprising thing is that it should have taken us so long to discover these examples of tool-using. The Egyptian vulture is a very well-known bird, and it has been well-known for thousands of years. Yet it was not until 1966 that Jane Goodall noticed that when this vulture wants to break open an ostrich egg it either throws it at a rock, or at another egg, or throws a stone at it. The vulture will search around over a distance of about fifty yards if necessary, to find a suitable stone. It will then fly back with the stone in its bill, and sling it with a violent movement of the head. It will repeat this until the shell is cracked. One vulture even threw a rock weighing two pounds, and continued to do so for some time.

Since it has so often happened that an animal's use of a tool has been overlooked for a very long time, it could well be that there are many more tool-users yet to be discovered.

Egyptian vulture cracking open an ostrich egg

When Elephants Purr

IT SOUNDS almost too ridiculous to talk about the tummy rumblings of elephants. All the same, they puzzled big-game hunters in the early part of this century. Then, when naturalists went shooting elephants with cameras, they also had something to say about the tummy rumblings. What they were all agreed upon was the surprising way the elephants could control them. There might be a herd of elephants feeding in the bush, each one rumbling noisily away, yet, as soon as the hunter or the naturalist drew near, all these noises would stop almost at once.

Only quite recently has it been discovered that these sounds come from the elephant's vocal cords. Should an elephant, while feeding, find itself hidden from its fellows it starts this rumbling sound in its throat, the noise reverberating throughout its massive body.

It is something like the purr of a cat, a sound made in the throat that seems to come from the tummy.

So long as elephants are hidden from each other they keep in touch by this "purring". It gives each animal a feeling of security because even if it cannot see another elephant, it knows from these sounds it is not alone. There is, however, another value to it. Should an elephant see, hear or smell danger approaching it stops purring. The other elephants around it know this is a danger signal, and they stop also. So the alarm is spread throughout the herd putting each member on the alert.

While elephants are in the open each can see what the others are doing. They can also watch the approach of danger, whether it is a lion or a man. It is only when they are among thick cover that their "tummy-rumblings" are used.

African elephants at an artificial waterhole

JANE BURTON

Ocean-Hopping Egrets

ONE OF the great advantages of being able to fly, as we have found since the aeroplane was invented, is that you can cover long distances in a short space of time. A hundred years ago there were plenty of people who had never in their lifetime been farther than the next village. Today you are behind the times if you have passed the age of twenty and not been halfway round the world. Only bats, insects and birds among animals (as well as the extinct reptiles known as pterodactyls) have achieved true flight. But there are plenty of others that have learned to glide, such as the flying squirrels. There is even a freshwater flying fish that can leap out of water and fly for a few feet by flapping its front fins. These apart, it is only bats, insects and birds that truly fly.

The most spectacular air journey is that made by the arctic tern, which spends the northern summer in the Arctic and the southern summer in the Antarctic and travels 22,000 miles there and back, each year. Another bird, the cattle egret, has almost as striking a record as the arctic tern but in a different way. There are many kinds of herons known as egrets and this is a smallish one, white with a yellow bill, which lived originally only in Africa. Other herons feed in shallow water, on frogs and fishes. This one lives on land and feeds on insects in grassland. It also follows large hoofed animals, such as

The cattle egret that originated in Africa

cattle and antelopes, eating the insects that fly up from the grass as it is disturbed by their hoofs. Today the cattle egret has spread all round the world and it has done so under its own steam and in a fairly short space of time.

Nobody knows quite when it started to happen but the first move came when some cattle egrets landed in Australia, having made a journey of well over 5,000 miles. There are islands in between so the journey need not have been non-stop. At all events, cattle egrets did suddenly appear in Australia after Europeans had settled there, and from Australia cattle egrets occasionally make another hop, to New Zealand. Other cattle egrets suddenly appeared

Cattle egrets waiting to catch insects disturbed in the grass by the elephant's hoofs

in South America, probably in the 19th century, although the first firm record we have is of one shot in Guyana in 1937 and preserved in the museum there. The first record of these birds breeding in America was in 1950 but before that they had spread north to Florida, in 1941 or 1942, and they have now spread north as far as southern Canada.

A common egret was once found on the subantarctic island of South Georgia, having travelled from South America 1,600 miles away. Weather records show that there had been strong winds for several days that could have helped the bird's long distance flight. No doubt strong winds have helped the cattle egret in its spread. But what helps it to colonize the new lands? In America, at least, forests have been cleared and swamps, where other herons fed, have been drained to make grasslands for cattle. In Australia grasslands were cultivated and cattle imported. So in both places man had made, for his own purposes, the ideal conditions for the cattle egret and had driven out the other herons by depriving them of the shallow water with its frogs and fishes.

Saving the Oryx

THE ARABIAN peninsula, lying between Africa and Persia, is largely desert but it is rich in oil wells. In the desert used to live the Arabian oryx, now almost wiped out because of the oil—in a rather curious way.

The Arabian oryx is a dainty gazelle, almost white, with chocolate markings on its legs and with long straight horns. At one time it ranged from Syria to Iraq, able to live in the endless sandy desert because it could find enough desert plants to eat and, more important, it could go for long periods without drinking. Because desert plants are few and far between an oryx had to travel far, fifty miles or more in a day. When the sun was hot it would dig away at the sand with its horns and hoofs to make a saucer in which it could lie shaded by a bush, or it would lie in a sand-dune, its colour blending with that of the sand so that it was hard to see.

To have killed an oryx was for the Arabs a mark of courage, endurance and skill. The hunter might have to track his quarry across the pitiless desert for a fortnight, by which time his own food and water would be giving out. Despite the difficulties of hunting them, the number of oryxes dropped steadily and by the end of the 19th century there

There are two other species of oryx, apart from the Arabian one, of which the Beisa oryx, shown here on the savannah in Kenya, more closely resembles the Arabian oryx

JANE BURTON

were only two parts of the peninsula where they could be found. Then came twin misfortunes: the invention of the motor-car and of automatic firearms and the world's need for oil.

Money for oil flowed into the Arab states. Europeans went in to help the Arabs to drill for oil and build the wells. Oil workers could afford cars and modern firearms, and the belief still held that it was a fine thing to kill an oryx. Now, however, it was easy. The motor-car could outpace the oryx, which could be sprayed with bullets, and more than one automobile could take part in the hunt. We are told that in one hunt 300 vehicles were spread out across the desert and the men in them shot at everything that moved.

By 1961 it was feared that the Arabian oryx was extinct, but this proved to be a false alarm. Nevertheless, the truth was that only a few hundred had survived and these were all living in one area. It became clear that unless something was done it would only be a matter of time before no more Arabian oryxes were left. In 1962 an expedition set out to try to capture some of them alive. The idea was to take them into captivity and find a suitable place somewhere else in the world, where they could be looked after, in the hope they would breed. The expedition was able to capture two males and one female, but they also brought back valuable information on the oryxes' way of life. In fact, there were already two breeding herds, one in Saudi Arabia and one in Qatar, both belonging to the rulers of

The last moments in the capture of an Arabian oryx before it was transported to the Phoenix Zoo where it will form part of a breeding herd which it is hoped will save the species from extinction

HUBERTUS KANUS

Beisa oryx are easily recognised by their distinctive facial markings

these countries. The oryxes remaining in the wild were given protection by the Sultan of Oman. The three oryxes captured were added to by King Saud of Saudi Arabia and the Sheikh of Kuwait, and by 1966 all these, now numbering eleven males and five females were taken to America, to the Phoenix Zoo in Arizona.

If, in years to come, the Arabian oryx becomes extinct in the wild and at the same time the herds in captivity flourish and increase greatly in numbers, some may be taken back to Arabia and set free, as has happened with the Hawaiian goose, or néné. This goose was in danger of being wiped out, so some were brought to the Wildfowl Trust at Slimbridge, Gloucestershire. From 25,000 the numbers of the goose

had slumped by 1950 to thirty-four, of which seventeen were in captivity. In the nick of time the wild ones were protected. Those in captivity were breeding so successfully that in 1962 it was possible to send back thirty-two by plane to Hawaii. During the next two years more were sent. There are now nearly a thousand, of which more than half are living wild (but still protected) in Hawaii.

Breeding geese is easier than breeding oryxes, but there is no reason why the Slimbridge success story cannot be repeated with the Arabian oryx and other rare species. Indeed, from being places of education and recreation, zoos are likely to become, more and more in the future, breeding places for rare species.

Phoenix Trees

PHOENIX is a town in Arizona, one of the south-western states of the U.S.A. There is much desert there so the climate should suit the oryx. Because of its name, Phoenix is a particularly appropriate zoo in which to revive a species.

The myth of the phoenix goes back to the earliest days of the Ancient Greeks, who learned of it in Egypt. This mysterious bird was said to come from the east every five years to Phoenicia, now the Lebanon. It settled in the palm trees, built a nest, set it on fire with sparks from the sun and was consumed in the flames. Three days later a new phoenix rose from the ashes. The oryx has not been reduced to ashes but it was near to extinction. We can only hope that at Phoenix Zoo it will "rise from its ashes" and come to life again.

The magnificent cedars of Lebanon, some of which are over 100 feet high

Curiously enough, this tenuous link between Phoenix and the Lebanon brings to mind another story of preservation. The Lebanon is the home of magnificent cedars, members of the pine family with massive trunks and huge spreading branches arranged in tiers. The largest are over 100 feet high. Their foliage is tufts of evergreen needles and on the branches are upright, barrel-shaped cones. The wood is hard and makes good timber. Solomon's temple was built of it and both then and since the wood was much in demand. Not only were mature trees cut down but goats, so much kept in the Middle Ages, ate the seedlings. So the once extensive forests gradually disappeared, until only a few thousand cedars were left. These are now protected, in the Cedars of Lebanon Reserve.

In the 17th and 18th centuries it was the fashion to plant this cedar in the gardens and parks of the well-to-do in Britain. It is said to live 500 years and today there are plenty here aged 300 years or more. Indeed, if we could make an accurate count we should probably find there are several times as many cedars as there are in the Lebanon.

Quite unwittingly, the rich people of several centuries ago did for the cedar of Lebanon what the International Union for the Conservation of Nature and the Fauna Preservation Society, in London, did for the Arabian oryx.

A common shrew investigates the contents of a bottle—at its peril

Litter-Traps

THERE is one first step we can all take in conservation and that is to refrain from throwing down litter. It is such a simple and easy thing to become a litter-bug by sheer thoughtlessness, and equally simple and easy to avoid.

Once I was walking up a hill in autumn. The slope was clad in trees and bushes in their autumn tints, and the ground was spangled with gaily coloured toadstools of many kinds. It was like walking in Elysian fields. Then, as I neared the brow of the hill, I began to see scraps of paper among the toadstools. The nearer I got to the brow the thicker was the litter. Yes, I had reached a famous beauty spot.

Shortly after this I visited a valley in Wales, said by some to be the most beautiful valley in Britain. The litter was frightful. My daughter, then a young girl, gashed her foot on a piece of broken bottle hidden in the grass.

I used to live on the edge of a wood. Cars could drive in for a hundred yards and their occupants could picnic. Ramblers, twenty or thirty at a time, would walk right through, having their lunch in the heart of the wood. Wherever cars could go was litter but you could never see where the ramblers had been. Why is it that so many motorists, able to take away their rubbish by merely putting it in the boot, leave so much behind, while ramblers carefully stow it in their rucksacks and carry it away?

Should you think litter does no harm, here is an interesting sideline on it. Several naturalists have, over the past few years, made a study of the mice, voles and shrews that have crawled into milk bottles thrown into hedges and have died in them. If the bottle is slanting upwards the animal can slide in but cannot climb out up the slippery glass slope. Even weasels have been trapped in milk bottles.

Also, if you don't enjoy mosquito bites, remember that these insects lay their eggs on water—even on the rain-water in the bottom of a tin can thrown into a hedge.

How Birds Keep Warm

The north wind doth blow,
And we shall have snow,
And what will poor robin do then?
    Poor thing.

You all know how the rest of the nursery rhyme gives the answer:

He'll sit in a barn,
And keep himself warm,
And hide his head under his wing.
    Poor thing.

But is the answer right? The first part may sometimes be correct, but often there are not enough barns for all the robins in the country, unless we packed them in very closely. The Jenny wren has no objection to sleeping packed like a sardine. Indeed, when the weather is cold the wren alters its habits. Instead of each going to its own roost the wrens in a district start to move around more than usual, making a special roosting call—drumming each other up, so to speak—then all make for one roosting place. Inside, in a very small space, the first arrivals form a circle on the floor of the cavity with their heads pointing towards the centre. Others following land on them, also in a circle with heads to middle; and there may be a third tier. We know this because someone opened a tit's nesting box, after seeing a whole lot of wrens fly in, and saw them arranged in this tidy heap. The record for numbers is fifty-two and was obtained by a man living in a thatched house. He noticed wrens flying in under the wire-netting stretched over the thatch to keep out sparrows. He watched them doing this several nights running and counted them.

Robins would not do this because they have such a strong territorial instinct. Most birds take over a territory in spring, the male choosing it and the female then joining him. They build a nest somewhere near the centre of this plot of land and drive out any of their own kind that trespass on it. As a rule, birds hold a territory only during the breeding seasons, but a robin holds its territory more or less throughout the year. If there were a barn a robin going in would probably drive out any other robin that tried to follow it.

So there are not enough barns to go round. There are, however, plenty of warm places, even if we do not count outhouses. There are bushes, especially evergreen bushes, where birds can roost. They have the shelter of the bush itself, which tends to keep out the cold, and also the bush itself gives out a little heat—not so much as in summer when it is actively growing, but enough to make a slight difference to the temperature inside.

Now we come to the second part of the answer given in the nursery rhyme. It is a strange thing that if you were to ask a hundred people where a bird puts

Robin in a snowy wood, and on a window ledge looking for crumbs

its head when it sleeps, almost certainly ninety nine of them, possibly the whole hundred, would say "under its wing". It is one of the fixed ideas we have, that a bird tucks its head under its wing when it sleeps. Yet in fact only penguins do this, and even they only manage to get the beak under the wing. Other birds, except for owls with their very short necks and large heads, tuck the beak and the front part of the head among the shoulder feathers. A penguin's feathers are too short even to tuck the bill among them.

So we can now ask: how do birds keep warm in cold weather, when they are not moving about? To begin with they have a layer of fat under the skin, like the blubber of a whale but nothing like so thick. Their feathers also keep the heat in because they trap a layer of air. If necessary a bird fluffs out its feathers and this increases the thickness of the

layer of air trapped, forming even better insulation. Provided a bird is well fed the fat and the feathers are enough to keep the warmth of the body in and to keep out the cold. But small birds cannot go long without food. This is why wrens clump, as it is called. They are merely huddling together to conserve heat.

A wren is three and three-quarter inches long, a robin five and a half inches; a wren weighs only one-third of an ounce, a robin three-quarters of an ounce. So a wren is much smaller than a robin, and this is very important when heat and cold are in question. The smaller an animal is, the larger, in proportion, is its surface to its volume. That is, it has a high surface area to volume ratio. The larger this ratio the more the body loses heat, so a small bird gets cold more quickly than a larger bird. It is the same with the furred

63

animals, or mammals. A shrew or a harvest mouse loses heat so quickly it cannot go more than three hours without food. So both these treat the twenty-four hours of day and night in quite a different way from us. They rest for three hours, then run about and feed for three hours, alternately throughout day and night. If a shrew is without food for four or five hours it dies of what is called cold starvation. That is, it is giving out so much heat all the time that it is using up the food in its stomach and the fat under its skin to keep warm. In the end it has no food inside its body either to keep out the cold or to use as energy to power its muscles.

When birds die in hard weather, it is because they cannot get enough food, or enough of the right kind. Birds kept in aviaries can stand even a hard winter out of doors, because they are well fed.

It is always surprising how parrots, whose native home is the tropics, can stand exposure to cold in temperate latitudes, provided they have plenty of food. The fact that they are given so much sunflower seed, containing plenty of oil, helps a great deal. Tropical birds in zoos can keep their temperature up at the normal 106°F when the air around is below freezing point if they are given enough of the right kind of food. It is often said you should bring guinea pigs indoors in winter. Possibly the guinea pigs might like to be coddled, but some people leave them outdoors throughout the year. Given plenty of the right food, as well as straw or hay in a box shelter, guinea pigs will not only survive our winters out-of-doors, but will grow a better coat and be in an altogether better condition.

Winter is a hard time for wild birds, but these blackbirds and thrushes have found a feast

JANE BURTON

Test Your Knowledge

The point about asking questions, even when the answers are easy to obtain, is to cause you to stop and think. Any kind of puzzle makes a change from straightforward reading and whets our curiosity—and a sense of curiosity is believed by some scientists to be the most compelling of all natural instincts in the higher animals.

1. What is epimeletic behaviour?
2. Can insects see colour?
3. A baby cat is called a kitten, a baby dog is a pup, a baby fox is a cub, a baby hare is a leveret: what is the proper name for a baby rabbit?
4. Is it true that a fungus can lasso worms?
5. Do you know why we speak of ducks when they are in a flock (sportsmen refer to a flock of duck), and why we then call a female a duck and a male a drake?
6. What is a living fossil?
7. Can dolphins think?

Now turn to page 87 for the answers.

Short-tailed and wandering albatrosses

Aerials Kill Albatrosses

MUCH is said and written today about the dangers to our wild life. Some of these dangers are difficult to avoid, as we shall see from the story of the albatrosses in the Pacific.

Albatrosses are large seabirds that spend most of their time flying well out over the oceans using air currents to glide for miles without a beat of the wings. They only come to land to nest, usually on oceanic islands. Some albatrosses are white with black wing tips, others are brown, and all look like large gulls except that they have a hooked bill with the nostrils opening through horny tubes on the top of it. The largest of these birds, the wandering albatross, may be eleven and a half feet across the spread wings.

There was an ancient superstition among ocean-going seamen described by the poet Coleridge in his *Lay of an Ancient Mariner* that it was unlucky to kill an albatross. Nevertheless, albatrosses have long suffered at the hands of man. If the seamen left them alone, others did not, and for centuries they have been killed for food and for their feathers. In the latter part of the 19th century, for example, albatrosses' feathers were much used for decorating ladies' hats and also for stuffing beds. Three species of albatross in the North Pacific were the worst hit, the short-tailed albatross suffering most of all. On top of this the short-tailed albatross came near disaster when the last remaining colony on the Island of Torishima was hit by volcanic eruptions in 1939 and again in 1941. The whole colony was exterminated except for a few birds that happened to be at sea. These have since been protected by the Japanese Government and the colony has started to pick up again.

The other two North Pacific species also suffered badly, but there were more of them and also they were protected earlier. The largest colony was on Laysan Island. This is one of a string of islands, over a thousand miles long, stretching from Midway Island to Hawaii, in the North Pacific. On Laysan, which is to the east of Midway, the slaughter was so terrible that in 1909 President Theodore Roosevelt declared this and other nearby islands a wild life reserve. Even this would not have helped very much had it not happened that the demand for albatross feathers for millinery died out.

Just as it looked as though the Pacific albatrosses were going to have an easier time there came the Second World War, which spread to the Pacific. Not only were hundreds of thousands killed merely in the ordinary course of men shooting at each other, they were also caught for food and on one island the starving Japanese soldiers killed and ate the whole colony.

This is not the worst of the story, because in 1935 Midway Island was chosen as a staging post for planes crossing the Pacific. As its name tells us, this island is in mid-Pacific, half-way between Asia and America. At first the planes had little effect on the albatrosses, but during the war that broke out in 1940, Midway was used for military aircraft and the number of runways on the island was increased considerably. Then came the invention of the jet plane. A bird being sucked into a jet engine can completely destroy it, and with albatrosses flying over a runway there is always the fear that this could happen when a plane is in the air.

In times of war people can give little thought to the effects on animals of the things they are doing. On Midway Island runways were needed urgently for the planes and these were built right across the ground where for thousands of years albatrosses had been breeding. A bird cannot change its habits overnight, so aeroplane and bird

Laysan albatrosses in the North Pacific

found themselves a daily danger to each other. Somebody suggested that the whole population of albatrosses on Midway should be destroyed. This would have meant killing off half a million of the Laysan albatrosses, or one third of their total number. Fortunately this was never done, but nevertheless, many thousands of the birds were killed in the attempt to control them.

All kinds of difficulties have arisen in trying to use Midway and the other islands for aeroplanes, while at the same time interfering as little as possible with the albatrosses. This can be illustrated by what happened on another island, Eastern Island, near Midway. As the man-made air traffic increased a forest of radio masts sprang up. Although albatrosses are so skilful in using air currents to glide over the oceans they are quite unable to manoeuvre easily in the air. As a result many fly into the radio masts or the cables holding them up, especially when strong winds drive them to where the masts are more numerous. After a storm hundreds of dead albatrosses litter the ground. In one year, in six months only, 3,000 albatrosses were killed in this way. This is only one of the many problems that arise as a result of man's progress in technology, and each one brings its particular difficulties to our wild life.

In recent years Laysan albatrosses have frequently had to face being slaughtered by man

Hooked on Humans

YOU SOMETIMES hear people talking about an animal being "fixated on human beings"; or they may say it is "human fixated". You will not find this explained in any dictionary because these terms have not had time to get into the dictionaries. They started to come into use about twenty years ago among people studying birds, because birds are particularly prone to becoming human fixated. The best way to explain the meaning of the phrase is to tell the story of my tame crow.

It was one of several birds which had been the pets of a medical student. He had reached the stage in his training when he had to work in a hospital and so could not look after his pets, and he

wanted me to take them over. The crow in question was one of two, both females, and I housed them in a very large aviary. The first thing I noticed about them was that every morning, as soon as I went into their aviary to put down their food and water, they would fly over to me, land at my feet, and invite me to stroke their heads. They were very jealous of each other and usually when I went to stroke one of them the other would attack it.

After I had had these two for a few years one of them escaped and was not seen again. A few black feathers near the aviary may have meant that a cat or a fox had taken it. The one left behind is therefore the one with which this story

A. W. BESLEY

Birds are very prone to becoming human fixated, and crows are no exception

is concerned. To start with, this hen crow very, very seldom crowed like a crow. What it did do, and all day long, was to make the sounds of children playing: crying, laughing, calling boisterously or petulantly. Indeed, people passing my garden, unable to see the crow, thought there were children playing in the garden. We can only suppose that this crow was hand-reared as a fledgling in a garden where children played.

Left on its own, this one hen crow would escape from its aviary from time to time. Often, the first I would know of this would be when the telephone bell rang and, lifting the receiver, I would hear a voice saying: "Have you lost a crow? There is one on my window-sill tapping at the window, and it won't go away." All I had to do then was to go round to my neighbour's house, go in and open the window, pick up the crow

and bring it home.

The crow did not always go to the same house, but it always did the same thing. Once free of the aviary it would fly around for a while, enjoying its new-found freedom, then it would settle on a window-sill of the house nearest it and tap the window to attract the attention of the person inside. If, however, I happened to be in the garden at the time it escaped, the first I would know of it would be when a large black bird settled near me and began to make childish noises.

After several years of this there came a time when a group of houses was built in the village. The children of the families that came to live in these houses caught the crow's attention the next time it escaped, and it flew down to them. I knew this after someone phoned me to ask if I had lost a crow. Ever since then, whenever the crow has escaped, it has flown straight to wherever the children may be playing. If, as sometimes happens, they are in school, the crow perches on a roof or on a garden fence as if waiting for them to appear.

Perhaps I should explain why the crow gets out, in case someone asks why I am so careless. With a very large aviary the wire-netting, over the years, gets loosened by the wind and a corner of it lifts, or it may rust at one point to leave a hole. The crow soon discovers these exits.

The interest here is that the crow is not only human fixated, it is even more fixated on children.

It might be asked, why not let the crow go free? I would do so except that

I should then have to spend all my time answering the telephone and going to fetch it back. There is another serious objection to this. A human fixated bird, because it has been hand-reared, has not learned to know its natural enemies. It is no more afraid of a cat or a fox than it is of a child. To give such a bird its liberty would be to sign its death warrant.

Elsewhere in this book we speak of breeding in zoos animals that are growing rare in the wild, and then setting their offspring free again. This has been done with the Hawaiian goose and it is being done with the orang utan. There is a danger, unless steps are taken to avert it, of these animals being human fixated and soon coming to grief when they are liberated. There is even a danger of wild animals being affected by this. Several years ago a young woman wrote to me from southern Africa. She told me how her father used to take her into the bush and teach her how to make friends with the small antelopes. But always, at the end of a meeting with a wild animal, he would throw a stone in its direction to make it run away. He explained that if one person taught a wild animal to be unafraid of people, the next person it met would probably want to kill it. So he took no chances.

Prickly Pest of Coral Reefs

THE CROWN-OF-THORNS starfish is up to two feet across. It has thirteen to seventeen arms and is covered with inch-long spines that are poisonous, so anyone treading on it with bare feet will feel pain as the poison spreads through his body. It is easy enough to tread on one of these starfishes because they are yellow and green in colour with greyish-blue on the surface of their arms, and their spines are tipped with red and orange. Amongst the living coral reefs, where the starfish lives, these colours are good camouflage.

The crown-of-thorns starfish feeds on the flesh of the coral. One of them will strip a square yard of coral bare in twenty-four hours, and a crowd of them will leave a trail of whitened coral, bare of flesh and dead, in a few days.

Until a few years ago nobody other than those who study starfishes—or those who had accidentally trodden on one—had ever heard of the crown-of-thorns starfish, yet it lived in all seas from the Red Sea through the Indian Ocean to the Great Barrier Reef of Australia and into the Pacific. Then, in 1968, it was noticed that the starfish had become very numerous and was beginning to destroy the coral reefs. In some places eighty to ninety per cent of the coral was being destroyed, while the numbers of the starfish had risen in places to 15,000 per acre.

One reason why the destruction of the coral reefs is regarded as a calamity is that it will have a far-reaching effect on other marine life. The waters of a coral reef are rich in food and oxygen so animal life of many kinds is crowded on the coral—sponges, anemones, worms, molluscs, barnacles, sea squirts and fishes. All these are interesting and some are unique. In wiping out the coral the starfish could do widespread damage to other things. On some Pacific islands this has a day-to-day importance, because the people living there depend so much on the fish they catch in the lagoons enclosed by the coral. Even if the fish are not wiped out they may become poisonous, because seaweeds grow over the dead coral and fish eating some of these are apt to get a poison in their flesh. Cases of food poisoning in Queensland, Australia, are believed to have been due to people eating fish caught off the Great Barrier Reef, where the starfish has been at work.

The population explosion of the crown-of-thorns starfish may be the result of human interference. Nobody can be quite sure of this, but it does seem as if the damage it does is greatest where people are living. Can it be the result of pollution—from sewage, perhaps? It may be that this kills off the small swimming animals that feed on the starfish larvae. Or is it because where people live on the coast they bathe, and in warm seas bathers must be protected from sharks, so sharks are killed? In spite of the starfishes' formidable spines they are eaten by certain sharks. Another of the starfish's enemies is the triton or trumpet shell, a large sea snail. Its shell, called a conch (pronounced conk), is collected by visitors to the shores. The fewer tritons there are, the fewer starfishes will be killed.

It is easy to see how one or two events, apparently trivial in themselves, lead to such an explosion. Some starfishes lay tens of thousands of eggs a year, others lay several millions in a season. We are not certain how many eggs a female crown-of-thorns starfish lays but let us suppose it is only 10,000 a

A prickly crown-of-thorns starfish that can strip a square yard of coral bare in 24 hours

year. Then every female starfish allowed to live because a shark or a conch has been killed means 10,000 more larvae. If the enemies of the larvae are killed off by pollution, the number of young starfishes the following year may be ten or a thousand times more than normal. In no time at all, the sea-bed in some places could be running alive with young starfishes, all capable in a few years of growing to two feet across and eating up a square yard of coral flesh a day.

If we let our imagination run free we could picture tropical seas crowded with thorny starfishes eating up the coral, upsetting the natural balance, and behaving altogether like some evil plague. Clearly, the scientists studying this plague are baffled, and also worried. The report they issued in 1970 gives no sign that the starfish nuisance is abating. Nor does it give any hint that anyone is any nearer knowing the cause or the remedy for it.

To try killing the starfish with chemicals would endanger other marine life. In any event, to try to do this with an animal living 15,000 to the acre, in tropical seas stretching halfway round the globe, would be a far greater task than any Hercules attempted. What we have to hope for is that the nuisance of the starfish is less than we are led to believe—or, if not that, that it will right itself naturally before too much damage has been done. If not, it may be necessary to look for some natural control, such as another animal that can be encouraged to prey on the starfish. Even that, at the moment, looks almost like asking for the moon.

Whistling in the Dark

As FAR back as the 18th century an Italian scientist was trying to find out how bats were able to fly in the dark without crashing into things. An English scientist came very near to solving the mystery in 1926, but the real answer did not come until about 1940. Then, two American scientists found that the small insect-eating bats send out ultrasonic squeaks, above the range of the human ear, while flying. These are different to the squeaks they make while at rest, which we can hear. There is a pause between the ultrasonic squeaks during which the bat listens for the echo. This tells it not only that there is an obstacle in its path but, from the time taken for the echo to reach its ears, how far away the object is. The method is known as echo-location, or sonar.

The story of bats' echo-location has been told so often that it is probably known to most people, at least in the simple form in which it is given here. Yet the more research that is done on it the more complicated it is seen to be. It is now clear that a bat flying about, giving out these pulses we cannot hear, is able to get an echo-picture of its surroundings just as we get a sight-picture.

As the research on bats progressed, more refined instruments were devised. Moreover, scientists began to turn their attention to other animals, and they found bats were not the only ones to use ultrasonics. One of the next animals to catch their attention was the bottle-nosed dolphin. This is the dolphin so well known for its antics in seaquaria, the large concrete tanks filled with sea water. It now seems certain that dolphins, porpoises and whales use a sonar, as it is now called,

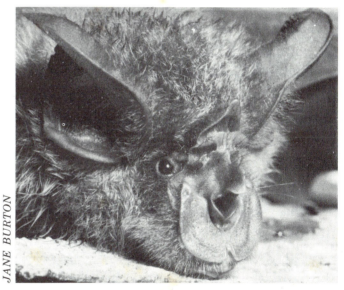

Horseshoe bat (above) and whiskered bat (below)

STEPHEN DALTON

Only comparatively recently has it been discovered that mice can hear ultrasonics

in much the same way as bats. It helps them to find their way about, when swimming at night or in murky waters. They also use it for finding their prey. How sensitive this sonar can be is shown by experiments in which a dolphin was offered a water-filled gelatine capsule and a fish the same size. Even when blindfolded the dolphin could tell the difference. In addition, dolphins use ultrasonics to talk to each other.

There are also two kinds of birds that use a sonar, but in their case, it is a sonic sonar. That is, the sounds they use are audible to our ears. One is the oilbird of South America, that spends the day in deep dark caves and comes out at night to feed on fruit. It uses its sonar only for finding its way about in the caves. The other birds are the cave swiftlets of South-East Asia, whose nests are collected for birds'-nest soup. They too use sonar for flying around in the dark caves where they nest.

Other animals now known to use ultrasonic sonar are mice, voles and shrews. In several instances the discovery that a particular mouse or shrew uses sonar was accidental, as the discovery came when they were being studied for other purposes. Before 1940, the things these animals did would have aroused no suspicion. Now, with the knowledge of how bats use ultrasonics in mind, scientists are on the look-out and make the necessary tests. For example, one scientist was trying to photograph a house mouse in a glass cage. The mouse simply squatted huddled in a corner of the cage. To try to make the mouse move about, without frightening it, the scientist rubbed his finger over the glass. He noticed that as he did so the mouse moved its ears in time with his finger. He tried again and again, and it became obvious the mouse could hear sounds made by his finger which he himself could not hear. Possibly these were ultrasonic, so tests were made which showed the mouse could hear ultrasonics.

When another scientist was testing the intelligence of shrews he was struck by the way they seemed able to avoid solid objects in semi-darkness, although they have very small eyes and poor eyesight. Again, using the new instruments, he was able to show that shrews use ultrasonics as bats do but in a less skilled manner.

Some animals can hear ultrasonics but do not themselves make ultrasonic sounds. A dog can hear the Galton whistle, the silent whistle, as it is called, which gives a whistle above the range of the human ear. Cats can hear ultrasonics; in fact, they hear high notes better than low notes. This is why a cat will come more quickly when a woman calls it than when a man calls it. Probably dogs and cats use ultrasonic hearing to listen for the animals they prey upon, just as an owl can hear and identify the ultrasonics given out by a mouse in the grass.

We are not yet sure whether mice talk to each other in ultrasonics but this is highly likely. One of the latest discoveries is that baby mice call to their mothers in ultrasonics. A human baby screams its head off when it is hungry or afraid. A baby mouse does the same thing but in ultrasonics, so we do not hear it. And where the human mother answers her baby in words we can hear, the mother mouse answers in ultrasonics. Probably a cat would hear both the babies and the mother mouse.

An eagle owl, having heard the mouse's ultrasonics, swoops down on its prey

Playful—or Merely Stupid?

PEOPLE have long noted that gulls will fly up with a mussel or a cockle in the bill to a height of about thirty feet and then let the mollusc fall. Crows on the seashore will do the same. Often the shellfish will fall on to a rock and be smashed, and the bird can then eat the soft body inside. At other times a bird drops a shellfish on sand, which cushions its fall. The bird then swoops down, picks up the shellfish and repeats this a number of times before giving up. At least, that is what it looks like. So we say that birds have not the sense to know whether they are dropping the shellfish on rock and will stupidly keep on trying on sand even when it is useless. But is this really so?

Gulls have also been seen stealing

A tern carrying a captured crab

eggs in the breeding season. A gull will steal an egg from another bird's nest, fly up with it, drop the egg, swoop and catch it in mid-air, fly up and drop it again, repeating this until it misses and the egg smashes on the rocks below. Then it flies off and steals another egg and repeats the process. We call this play, because that is what it looks like, since the gull does not necessarily eat the smashed egg.

Terns are sea-birds related to gulls. They usually work over water, and they have also been seen to do something very similar. When they miss, however, their "plaything" falls into the water and sinks, so it is often difficult to find out what it was the tern was carrying. On one occasion a tern was seen carrying a crab in its bill, which it dropped, swooped and recaptured several times, each time with a quick snap of the bill. It did this very many times, and the observer concluded that the tern was deliberately trying to break the crab's shell, by taking several bites at it. But terns will do the same with a small fish, which does not need cracking.

Here, then, is a first-class puzzle. Several kinds of birds are doing much the same thing but we ascribe different motives to them. Is it always play, or do they do the same thing from different motives at different times? Nobody knows the answer, but it is a nice problem to think about.

The Old Man of the Woods

DURING the last ten years the two African apes, the chimpanzee and the gorilla, have been closely studied in their wild state. There have been magazine articles about them and several books have been written on them. We know more about them than ever before. One thing these studies have taught us is that the gorilla, far from being the ferocious killer that has often been presented to us in films, is a peaceful animal that does not know its own strength. There is, however, a third manlike ape about which we hear very little—the orang-utan.

The orang is four feet tall, with arms so long they reach almost to its ankles when it stands upright. It is covered with long russet brown hair and its face is, in many ways, very human. Because of this it is often known as "the old man of the woods". The orang lives in certain kinds of forest in Borneo and Sumatra, swinging through the trees with its long arms, sleeping each night on a platform of branches in a fork of a tree and feeding especially on a fruit known as durian.

At one time orangs lived over a wide area of South-East Asia, as far north as southern China and northern India. We know this because in these areas their teeth are often found in the ground (all that is left of their skeleton). But for a long time now orangs have been found only in Borneo and Sumatra. This suggests at once that they are a dying race, and in fact since the Second

How could anyone refuse this orang-utan . . . ?

The "old man of the woods" fascinated by a piece of metal tubing

World War their numbers have been steadily dropping. Now there are probably no more than 5,000 in the world.

On the two islands where orangs now live human beings are increasing in numbers, as they are elsewhere in the world. There is need for more land to grow crops. Money is also needed, and the forests contain valuable timber. So the forests where the orangs live are being steadily cut down, for timber, and the ground cleared for crops. Any orangs seen are likely to be shot, or at best driven from their homes. Young orangs, on the other hand, may be captured and end up in zoos.

There is, indeed, a big demand for orangs for zoos and, as always happens when the demand is high, the prices paid are also high. This tempts people to go looking for the animals to sell to dealers, who then sell to zoos all over the world. Orangs are especially vulnerable. They have little fear of humans, being more curious about them than anything else, so the hunter can quite easily get close to them. Any that do move away are driven into an isolated tree and the tree is then felled; or else men surround it, along with their dogs, and after a few days the poor orang is forced through hunger and thirst to come down.

What these hunters are after are the young animals, which makes matters even worse. To capture a young orang may mean that the hunter must shoot the mother first. The youngster is then taken across the sea, to Singapore or Bangkok, where there are always dealers waiting to buy. On the journey many orangs die. In fact, probably two out of three young orangs captured die before they reach a zoo, for they are prone to disease when they lack their main food, the fruit of the durian tree.

Largely through the efforts of Tom and Barbara Harrisson, living in Sarawak and working through the International Union for the Conservation of Nature, attempts have been made to stop the illicit traffic in orangs. Wherever possible government officials confiscate any captured young orangs. Today most zoos refuse to buy orangs obtained in this way, but the smuggling still goes on because there are still some zoos that will buy them.

It is not as though orangs have large

families. A female orang has only one baby at a time, and she gives birth only once in every four years. Added to this, two out of every five baby orangs born die before they are weaned.

There is an urgent need for a large tract of forest to be set aside as a permanent home for orangs. The trouble is that where the orangs live is far from large towns, so policing such a reserve would be difficult. And we have to remember that the local peoples living near the forests where orangs are to be found have always been hunters. They see no wrong in killing animals, even if these animals happen to be man's first cousins. Meanwhile, all that can be done is being done. Young orangs rescued from poachers and dealers are being cared for and, as soon as possible, taken back to the forests and set free. Even this brings its problems.

To begin with, most orangs rescued are in poor condition, and have to be carefully tended. In the course of this they become attached to their attendants—or as we say, fixated on humans (which you can read more about on p. 69). In fact, some orangs become so attached they grow jealous when they see an attendant feeding or handling another orang. They then become violent or go into tantrums. In some instances, too, the mere fact of having been in captivity leaves its own mark. One orang, kept in a cage so small it could hardly turn round, had become flat-footed, and the muscles of its hands were so wasted that it could not move its fingers properly. When released from its cage it was like a baby, squatting on the ground and pushing itself along with its hands.

A female orang, having been kept chained, felt unsafe when the chain was taken off. She refused to go to sleep at night unless the chain was put on her. Another orang had grown too fond of beer and whisky, and had also developed a craving for tobacco. Any smoker who went near it was in danger of having his cigarette snatched from his lips.

Since orangs are so like humans they do not need to be in captivity for long before they begin to behave more like humans than like wild apes. One orang watched men cutting and carrying wood and when, at the end of the day, the men stopped work the ape tried to carry on with what they had been doing. So, as you can see, the people who are looking after the rescued orangs have to train them to be wild orangs before releasing them once more, and this is much more difficult than trying to teach them human tricks.

For this orang-utan at least, life in the zoo is bliss

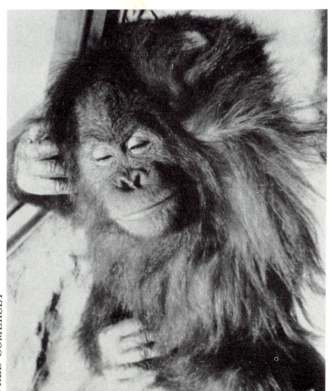

FRED SOMERSET

81

White whales, once nick-named "sea canary" because they make sounds like birds singing

Humpback Minstrels

LESS than twenty years ago one of our most distinguished zoologists stated in one of his books that "whales are not known to have any voice". He explained that they make a loud puffing sound when they blow and that in some kinds of whales this gives a tinny noise. He also added that some whales and dolphins were said to make a high-pitched whistling when under water. This scientist was himself an expert on whales. What he wrote then, in 1952, compared with the latest discovery, shows just how fast things can move in scientific research.

To take the story further back in time, for a long time whalers had nick-named the white whale (or beluga) of the North Atlantic the "sea-canary". They claimed that it made sounds like a

bird singing. If they were right then whales, dolphins and porpoises could not only use ultrasonics, they were also able to make sonics, that is sounds within the range of the human ear. Already, in 1949, it was becoming obvious that dolphins could both make ultrasonic sounds and hear them. As we have seen elsewhere in this book, much research has since been done to prove this is so. But was the name "sea-canary" justified?

About the time the distinguished zoologist was writing his book some scientists on a ship in the St. Lawrence River, in Canada, saw a school of white whales swimming around. They lowered underwater hydrophones into the water and to their surprise heard something resembling a mass meeting of village gossips, or one of those discussion groups on television when everyone gets excited. They could hear murmurings, gurglings, cluckings, chattering, hooting, whistling and many other sounds: not a bad performance for animals without a voice. In the years that followed the US Navy Department made recordings of the sounds made by whales.

The very latest comes as quite a surprise on top of these earlier surprises. Two American scientists have been studying the large humpback whale and they declare it to be remarkably musical. A musician, hearing the records they made, used them as a basis for a concerto which he called "And God created Great Whales". This was first played by the New York Philharmonic Orchestra in the summer of 1970. The songs of the humpback are said to rival the songs of birds but to last much longer. The songs of most birds last only a few seconds. A humpback "sings" for anything from seven minutes to half an hour. Moreover, each whale seems to have its individual tune, so we can only suppose they sing to keep in touch as they wander about below the surface, rather as the elephants make their tummy rumblings. There are some "songs" of the humpback whale that can be heard hundreds of miles away, we are told.

The humpback whale may be nearly fifty feet long when fully grown. It can be recognized by its humpback appearance as it leaps playfully out of the water, by the knobs on its head and flippers, and by its unusually long flippers. When courting, these whales are said to slap each other with their flippers, the slaps being so loud they can be heard a mile away.

Unfortunately, this playful musical whale which roams the seven seas is becoming rare. So many have been killed by whalers in the last ten years that their numbers are dropping fast.

Mistletoe Survey

ANYONE will tell you that in Britain mistletoe grows on apple trees and on oaks. This is what all the books say. Yet you can travel miles looking at every oak you can find and almost certainly you will not find even a small sprig of mistletoe. The Druids are said to have held the oak sacred and to have cut the mistletoe from the oak for their festivals. Perhaps this is why it is never, or hardly ever, found on oak trees to-day. In many parts of the country you never see it on the apple trees either. Instead, you may find it in plenty on the tall limes. Near Goodwood, in Sussex, there is a long grove of tall lime trees and on their bare branches in winter,

Mistletoe grows plentifully like this in most parts of England

high up in the trees, are large masses of mistletoe, several to each tree. In other places in southern England there is plenty of mistletoe on the limes and on nothing else, except occasionally the hawthorn.

A survey has been started to find out how much mistletoe there is, where it grows and on what trees. People in all parts of the country have been asked by the Botanical Society of the British Isles to join in this mistletoe count. When the work is done we may know much more about mistletoe than ever before.

Mistletoe is a semi-parasite. It is a green plant, so it can manufacture some of its own food. The seeds are carried to the branches of trees by birds, who wipe their beaks on the branches to get rid of these sticky objects. When the seeds germinate they send false-roots, known as haustoria—mistletoe has no true roots—down into the sap vessels in the wood, but they do little harm to the trees.

In some parts of England there is no mistletoe on the apple trees in large orchards because the fruit farmer cuts it off whenever he sees it. In the Midlands, and the western counties beyond, there is plenty of mistletoe. The fruit farmers treat it as a second crop, in addition to their apples, and it is from them we get the supplies that reach the shops at Christmas-time.

The Flourishing Fulmar

THE FULMAR is a sea-bird related to the albatross. Its name means "foul-mew" or "foul-gull". This name is partly because of its musky smell, but particularly because of its habit of spitting an evil-smelling oil from its stomach at anyone who disturbs it, to a distance of three to four feet. The fulmar looks like a gull when perched on the cliffs and like an albatross when flying. Like an albatross its nostrils are enclosed in a tube on the top of its bill, which is why we call these birds "tube-noses".

Until 1750 there were only two fulmar colonies in the North Atlantic: one on the island of St. Kilda and another larger colony in the Arctic, in the north of Iceland. St. Kilda is one of a group of very small islands well out in the Atlantic from the Outer Hebrides, off the west coast of Scotland. For 250 years fulmars spread only slightly from these two places. Then, in 1878, a small colony suddenly settled on the Faeroe Islands and another on the Kame, a cliff 1,200 feet high on the Shetland island of Foula. We do not know whether they were fulmars from St. Kilda or from Iceland. From then on the fulmars spread rapidly, first round the coasts of the British Isles, then to Norway in 1921. Southwards, they crossed the Channel to Brittany in 1960. Meanwhile they had spread to Greenland and Nova Scotia, and to the east they spread to the White Sea and also into the Baltic.

This represents a tremendous spread in the course of a hundred years, and it seems man is responsible for it. It is probable that the fulmars' original food consisted of the small animals swimming near the sea's surface, such as small fish, squid and even jellyfishes. They possibly also ate any small dead animals floating at the surface, and took pickings from dead whales and seals. Then, in the 17th century when whaling spread to the Arctic, there opened up a golden age for the fulmars. Wherever a whale was being cut up they gathered to feed on the pieces of blubber and flesh. They also scavenged the

A fulmar in Ireland on its nest

scraps from the ships' galleys. Altogether they had an almost unlimited supply of food and their numbers rose as a result.

When whaling died out, after the big whales in the Arctic had been more or less exterminated, the now very numerous fulmars had to look elsewhere for a living. They began to follow the fishing fleets, for the fish offal being thrown overboard.

There are few enemies prepared to face being sprayed with oil, and with so much food around the chicks were unlikely to go hungry. The main enemy was man, who scaled the cliffs to get the eggs and also to catch the parent birds for food. In 1930 all the people on St. Kilda were evacuated, so the fulmars there were left alone. In other places they were left unmolested from 1940 onwards, when it was found that fulmars could carry psittacosis, or parrot-disease.

Fulmars may live to the age of twenty five years and although each female lays only one egg a year, she starts when she is about seven to eight years old, so she will lay seventeen to eighteen eggs in her lifetime. If only four of these were to survive to breed, and the same happened throughout the colony, the population would double every twenty five years. Its actual rate of increase is probably even greater, thanks to the whalers and fishermen.

Two fulmars resent the intrusion of their neighbour

F. GREENAWAY

86

How Much Did You Know?

Here are the answers to the questions asked on page 65

1. "Epimeletic" is from a Greek word meaning "careful". When animals care for each other we speak of this as epimeletic behaviour. Until the present century everyone thought that only human beings could be Good Samaritans. Then a big game hunter in Africa, after shooting and wounding an elephant, saw two of its companions close in to support it into the bush. Another hunter who had killed an elephant saw the rest of the herd close in on it, lift it and carry it away. Curious to see what would happen, he followed. All through the night the elephants dragged their dead companion away, presumably until they realized it was useless.

Since then otters have been seen helping an injured companion away, supporting it one either side. And there have been other examples. Perhaps the best instance of epimeletic behaviour occurred in the common dolphin. In 1969 a research ship wanted a dolphin for study purposes, and one was harpooned. Six of its fellow dolphins at once came to the rescue. They lifted the injured dolphin twice to the surface so that it could take in air, but after that rescuers and rescued were lost to sight. We can only hope their first aid was successful.

2. Some insects have no colour vision, but many, especially those like bees and butterflies that visit flowers, can see colours. The range of colours they can distinguish is, however, different from ours. The wavelengths that produce the sensation of red in our eyes have little or no effect on insects' eyes. Where we see red, they see only blackness. They can, however, see ultra-violet, so they see colours and patterns we fail to see.

The male brimstone butterfly, one of the first butterflies on the wing in spring in Britain and Europe, looks yellow to us. To insects, able to see ultra-violet, the male brimstone is not just plain yellow but has a pattern, where patches on the wings reflect ultra-violet light.

Silverweed photographed in visible light (above) and ultra-violet light (below)

3. A baby rabbit is, strictly speaking, a rabbit, and it comes about in this way. The Latin for a rabbit is *cuniculus*, and the Romans had much to do with spreading the rabbit across Europe from Spain. As a result the name for it in many European languages is some form of the Latin. In modern Italian it is *coniglio*, in Spanish *coneja*, in Portuguese *coelho*, in Dutch *konijn* and so on. The Old French was *connin*, while the Old English was *conyng* or *coney*. Indeed, the laws of England used to speak, and still do, of conies, and people caught poaching rabbits were accused of "taking conies". In heraldry, also, a rabbit is called a coney. You will find in the Bible a reference to conies, but in fact this refers to the rock hyrax, a tiny relative of the elephant. When the Bible was first translated into English most people knew nothing about hyraxes so the translators called them conies.

Originally, a baby coney was called a rabbit, from the northern French or Walloon name *robett*, and the use of this name for the adult dates from the middle of the 19th century only.

4. As you know, a mushroom is a fungus and so is a toadstool. But these are only fruiting bodies, the parts that bear the spores. The real fungus is slender white threads that spread underground or in rotten wood.

There are several fungi that live in the soil and feed on very small, slender worms known as eelworms. Some of these fungi form sticky threads which trap the eelworms. Others form nets, almost like spider-webs. The most remarkable are those that form lasso rings made up of three cells only. In fact, these fungi can feed quite happily on other things and only form rings when there is an eelworm nearby. Some chemical given out by the eelworm excites the cells of which the rings are made. Under the microscope you can actually see the granules in the protoplasm of these cells beginning to dance. Then the ring grows out. The eelworm pushes through the ring and gets wedged; or the ring may suddenly expand inwards, gripping the eelworm, which struggles until it is dead. After this the threads grow into the eelworm and devour it.

5. The word "duck" was used for this waterfowl in the 12th century, simply because it "ducked" its head to feed. It was not until 300 years later that the word "drake" crept into use for the male.

Nobody knows why this happened except that the English language is such a mixture of European and native words. A good example of how such a mix-up can occur can be seen in the Isle of Wight, where there is a road called Rew Street. In Norman times it was called the Rue and as time passed the word "street" was added. We can only suppose people had forgotten that "rue" meant "street".

This, of course, does not explain how "duck" and "drake" came to be used, but it helps us understand how the mix-up could have occurred.

A mallard drake (above) and duck (below)

The tuatara of New Zealand

6. Dragonflies are, in a sense, living fossils. Their giant ancestors, up to two and a half feet across the wings, flew among the tree ferns of 300 million years ago. But they are not living fossils in the strictest meaning of the term. It is when we have a single species only, that has outlived all its relatives, that we speak of a living fossil.

The tuatara of New Zealand, which looks like a prehistoric lizard, is a living fossil. There were lots of its relatives living 150 million years ago, but about 70 million years ago they all died out, leaving only the tuatara. This is now found on only a few small islands in Cook Strait, between the North and South Islands of New Zealand.

Charles Darwin was the first to use the term living fossil. He applied it to the ginkgo or maidenhair tree, which has leaves shaped like those of the maidenhair fern, but much larger. The tree itself grows to sixty feet or more. It is a native of Japan and China but it was introduced into England in 1764 and is still often seen in gardens. Millions of years ago there were many kinds of ginkgo, but all have died out except this one species.

7. The first scientist to study the brain of a dolphin noticed it was large in proportion to the body, and that its surface was much folded, as in the human brain. But it was not until dolphins were kept alive in large aquaria, in the 1940's, that we began to appreciate their intelligence.

When a baby whale or dolphin is born it must straight away rise to the surface to take in air through its blowhole. Should it fail to do this, its mother will lift it to the surface with her snout, or by gripping one of its flippers with her teeth. Female dolphins will do the same with an injured companion.

It is almost as if the dolphins think it out, like the female dolphin whose baby was stillborn. She held it at the surface for a long time, as if hoping she would be able to bring it back to life.

One of the best stories concerns a dolphin of the kind known as the false killer whale which was in a large aquarium. An attendant in a diving suit went in to capture a smaller dolphin. As he held it in his arms the false killer nudged it free with its snout. The attendant caught the small dolphin again and held it more firmly. The false killer, finding it could not dislodge the smaller dolphin, gently nipped the attendant's leg with its teeth, as if to say "Let it go, or else . . . !"

The golden eagle—now a rare sight in Europe

How to Help

FROM time to time I receive a letter from a young person asking what they can do to help animals. These boys and girls have read or heard of the dangers facing our wild life and, because their hearts are in the right place, they want to do something about it. So, naturally, I would like to help them; but that is not easy.

Anything you or I do to help cannot make a great deal of difference, the problem being such a vast one. Nevertheless, every little does help. But to anyone living in a large town the chance of doing even this very little must seem fairly hopeless. Those living in the country, or in a country town, are better placed. They probably have a local natural history society they can join, or a county naturalists' trust. In any case, there is the Youth Service of the World Wildlife Fund, and the Conservation Corps run by the Council

for Nature. Having said this, I then have to leave it to the boys and girls to explore for themselves the particular ways in which they can help. Above all—and this is something I always stress—each of us should learn as much as possible about animals and wild life generally, because the biggest danger to our environment lies in ignorance. Let us take one striking example.

Eagles have been especially badly hit in many parts of the world because they are supposed to kill lambs or game. Among those most severely attacked have been the golden eagle and the sea eagle in Europe (including the British Isles); the wedge-tailed eagle of Australia; Verreaux's eagle and the martial eagle in Africa; and the golden eagle and the bald-headed eagle in North America. In Britain the sea eagle was exterminated early in this century.

In fact, eagles can be beneficial

because they feed so largely on animals we consider to be vermin. They kill hares that eat grass. They kill foxes that might kill lambs. And they eat other animals and birds that indirectly affect sheep or game preserves.

A golden eagle needs nine ounces of meat a day. A pair with their youngsters eat about 600 pounds of flesh a year. During the winter and spring they eat mostly the flesh of deer and sheep that have died from hard weather. The eagle family hunt over an area of 11,000 acres, and if they were to kill two or three lambs this would hardly be noticed from among the large number of sheep grazing such an area. Moreover, even this loss would be offset by the good they do in killing off the enemies of the sheep.

You may not be able to convince a shepherd, who has actually seen an eagle fly off with one of his lambs, that eagles should not be shot at sight. The important thing is that you yourself should be satisfied on the point.

Each one of us is a member of the general public, and the opinions we hold make up public opinion. Not long ago some people in Spain, belonging to the Basque country, were sentenced to death. There were many protests and the men were reprieved. At the same time some Jews in Leningrad were due to be executed because, it was said, they had tried to hijack a plane. They were reprieved. Both were the result of world public opinion making itself felt.

Public opinion is a very powerful weapon, especially when it is based on real knowledge. In one place in southern England, several years ago, the local council sent their workmen to cut down the scrub on a hillside. Their idea was a perfectly good one. It was to give people a clearer view of the valley below. They had overlooked, or did not know, that the scrub was one of the few places where nightingales nested each year. It so happened that a man was passing who belonged to the local natural history society. Having learned what the workmen were going to do, he went round to other members of the natural history societies. There were a few phone calls and the work was stopped while the plan was discussed. Eventually the scrub was cleared in places, but only where the nightingales did not nest, and everyone was satisfied.

There are, of course, times when direct action is called for.

One morning, about twenty years ago, I received a telegram from a lady in Hertfordshire. A pest officer had called on her to destroy the foxes living on her land. She had flatly refused him access and he had said he would call again the following day. She was asking me, in the telegram, if she could continue to refuse him access.

I telephoned my friend at the Ministry of Agriculture, who told me that if the foxes were on private land the owner could refuse to have them destroyed. I then phoned the lady who was most grateful and said: "If ever you are passing this way, do call and see my foxes."

Some weeks later I was passing that way and I made a point of driving over to her house. She owned eleven acres of land on which she had a goose farm—

92

and a family of foxes.

She told me the foxes had not interfered with the geese, so every day she put out two goose eggs for them. Moreover, she invited me to stay to see them. When it was dark she went to her back porch, switched on the light, put two goose eggs on the ground, called out "It's all right, you can come now", and then came indoors. Through the window I saw a fox come out of the bushes about 30 feet away, walk up to the porch and walk back to the bushes with a goose egg in its mouth. In a few moments it returned for the other egg.

While we were waiting for night to fall, we talked of this and that, and she told how on one occasion she met the local hunt at the five-barred gate by which one entered her property from the road. One man was about to open the gate. He explained they were going to draw her property, that is, hunt through it for foxes. She held the gate shut and forbade them to enter, and after a little argument they all departed.

The hunt followed the road round to where there was another five-barred gate leading into the goose farm. To their surprise, the lady was waiting for them, holding this gate shut also, and defying them to enter. She was so determined that in the end they left and never bothered her again.

Having told the story she then added, with a laugh, "I knew they were coming, but what they didn't know was that I had my horse saddled and ready, hidden behind the hedge. When they turned away I guessed they would try the other gate so I galloped across and got there before them."

Whether you agree with having foxes on your land, or whether or not you agree with fox-hunting, you must admit this lady had courage.

The respectful fox collects its supper . . .